T0360466

Diversity and Inclusion: Are We Nearly There Yet?

This book provides the first compact knowledge base on diversity & inclusion (D&I) targets in the UK screen industries. Drawing on new, in-depth industry research and progressive theoretical voices, the book will help readers understand what D&I targets are and what they could be in the future.

The book explains different types of D&I targets, how D&I targets are currently used and how they might be developed to strategically drive inclusion. D&I targets are an increasingly common feature of the screen industries, but there is little evidence and guidance on how to use them well. This book addresses that gap. The book offers, for the first time, a unifying terminology for D&I target setting in the UK screen industries, including for transorganisational D&I targets (targets set by one organisation for another). It is based on a cross-industry review of D&I target setting in the UK screen industries, using evidence from industry and academic research.

Providing a unique knowledge base on diversity & inclusion targets in the UK screen industries, this book will be of value to researchers, industry experts, practitioners, policy makers, campaigners and anyone who needs to understand D&I targets – to advise on them, to set and achieve them and to advocate for their effective, inclusive use.

Doris Ruth Eikhof is Professor of Cultural Economy & Policy at the University of Glasgow, UK.

Routledge Research in the Creative and Cultural Industries
Series Editor: Ruth Rentschler

This series brings together book-length original research in cultural and creative industries from a range of perspectives. Charting developments in contemporary cultural and creative industries thinking around the world, the series aims to shape the research agenda to reflect the expanding significance of the creative sector in a globalised world.

Cultural Work and Creative Subjectivity
Recentralising the Artist Critique and Social Networks in the Cultural Industries
Xin Gu

Advertising as a Creative Industry
Regime of Paradoxes
Izabela Derda

Professionalization in the Creative Sector
Policy, Collective Action, and Institutionalization
Edited by Margaret J. Wyszomirski and WoongJo Chang

Digital Transformation and Cultural Policies in Europe
Edited by Ole Marius Hylland and Jaka Primorac

Digital Transformation in the Recording Industry
Evolution of Power: From The Turntable To Blockchain
Anna Anetta Janowska

Diversity and Inclusion: Are We Nearly There Yet?
Target Setting in the Screen Industries
Doris Ruth Eikhof

For more information about this series, please visit: www.routledge.com/Routledge-Research-in-the-Creative-and-Cultural-Industries/book-series/RRCCI

Diversity and Inclusion: Are We Nearly There Yet?

Target Setting in the Screen Industries

Doris Ruth Eikhof

Routledge
Taylor & Francis Group

LONDON AND NEW YORK

First published 2024
by Routledge
4 Park Square, Milton Park, Abingdon, Oxon OX14 4RN

and by Routledge
605 Third Avenue, New York, NY 10158

Routledge is an imprint of the Taylor & Francis Group, an informa business

British Library Cataloguing-in-Publication Data
A catalogue record for this book is available from the British Library

ISBN: 978-1-032-56228-5 (hbk)
ISBN: 978-1-032-56230-8 (pbk)
ISBN: 978-1-003-43454-2 (ebk)

DOI: 10.4324/9781003434542

Typeset in Times New Roman
by Apex CoVantage, LLC

Contents

Foreword

Diversity and inclusion play a key role in the health and prosperity of the UK screen industries. In the last decade, we have gotten better at opening our screens and studios to a wealth of talents we had not recognised or even noticed before. We have learned to work more inclusively and to make screen careers more accessible and enjoyable. But we still have work to do. Too many systemic barriers are still in place, too much creativity and opportunity remain untapped. Too many people do not work in the UK screen industries who really should be part of our teams. In short, diversity and inclusion (D&I) continue to require our attention.

Targets are an important tool for creating more diverse and inclusive screen industries. D&I targets are already used extensively, including by ScreenSkills, the industry skills body for the UK screen industries. Screen-Skills sets D&I targets for itself and for its training providers, and it receives D&I targets from its funders.

In our work with D&I targets, we started coming across puzzling questions – about target setting processes, definitions, good practice guidance and unintended side effects. We worked with Professor Doris Ruth Eikhof from the University of Glasgow to better understand current practice within and beyond the screen industries and to build a framework for ScreenSkills' future D&I target setting.

The *ScreenSkills D&I Targets Review* found that the screen industries are generally ahead of many other sectors in working with D&I targets. It also found, though, overall:

- a lack of clarity in the language used to talk about D&I targets;
- a lack of consistency in the data used to set targets;
- a lack of transparency as to how or why particular targets are set;
- a lack of industry-wide sharing of learning and good practice.

The *ScreenSkills D&I Targets Review* has been useful in strengthening our own practice. We therefore decided to share what we learned. We wanted this new knowledge to be available to everyone so we can all improve effectiveness and accountability in working with D&I targets. And we wanted to foster conversation across the screen industries about D&I targets and inclusive behaviour: conversations about what we already do well and what we could do better, about the data we use and the information we provide.

In June 2023, ScreenSkills published the *D&I Targets Playbook*, a short, practical introduction to D&I targets based on the work of the *Review*. Some parts of the book you are reading right now are an extended version of that *Playbook*, providing greater detail of the research behind its practical suggestions. But this book goes beyond the work ScreenSkills commissioned. By drawing on Professor Eikhof's wider research and expertise, the final chapter of *Diversity and Inclusion: Are We Nearly There Yet?* also provides her thought-provoking ideas for the future.

Like the *Playbook* before it, *Diversity and Inclusion: Are We Nearly There Yet?* is an invitation. We are invited to see the opportunities we have and the change we can bring about. It shows us how we can use D&I targets to make our workplaces diverse, inclusive and welcoming, in the screen industries and beyond, and makes evidence-based recommendations to improve our practice. But by putting the carefully curated and analysed evidence from the *D&I Targets Review* into conversation with broader thoughts about diversity and inclusion, it also invites us to consider the paths that D&I targets can take us on and the destinations we may want to aim for. We may not always agree in the conversations that follow. However, I believe Professor Eikhof's insight can only help you and your organisation gain greater clarity and rigour in your approach. This belief stems from knowing that she has helped us.

Seetha Kumar, CEO, ScreenSkills

Acknowledgements

The most beautiful acknowledgement sections are those in which a gifted writer thanks the world for helping them birth their labour of love. Alas, writing this book was more an exercise in stubborn persistence, reminiscent of those final marathon kilometres during which my daughter held up a sign saying 'Turning back would be daft too'. It needed doing. But before every finish line lie countless steps, over sunny fields and driech pavements, and I want to thank those who took them with me. I hope I have done you all justice.

Chapters 2–4 of this book build on the *ScreenSkills D&I Targets Review* 2021–2022, and I am grateful to everyone involved in that project: To Beate Baldauf and Gaby Atfield for their initial review of the research and evidence; to the ScreenSkills Senior Management Team and all industry stakeholders for sharing their insights; to Jack Cortvriend and Caterina Branzanti for additional research support; to Deborah Williams and Neil Hatton for sense-checking the *D&I Targets Playbook* and to Sao Bui-Van and Creative Commons for making the *Playbook* look beautiful.

Terry Clague's editorial enthusiasm for my book proposal set an idea on the path to reality – the honorary #14 shirt remains yours. I am indebted to Christina Williams for her meticulous research support, admirable attention to detail and patience with my writing 'schedules' – I still don't know how you do it, Tina, thanks a million. Ranjit Blythe and Chris Pearce test-read the manuscript from a non-screen perspective – I'm grateful for your feedback and encouraging comments in just the right moment. The School of Culture & Creative Arts, University of Glasgow, supported my work on this book with an internal research award – thank you, Karen Lury, Mark Banks, Pauline McLachlan and Lisa Gallagher. Many thanks to Paula Clarke Bain, and to Naomi Round Cahalin and everyone at Routledge who turned files into an actual book.

Four people have been with this project all the way: Seetha Kumar commissioned the *ScreenSkills D&I Targets Review* and backed every step and stumble with leadership, foresight and conviction. Jeanette Berry navigated contracts and finances through an at times impenetrable administrative maze. Kevin Guyan read, commented and kept me believing that this little book had a place in the bigger picture we all need to paint together. Helen Shreeve brought an invaluable mix of project management skills, diplomacy, forensic reading and motivating discussions without which neither the *Review* nor this book would exist. My biggest thanks to all four of you for your support and for your tolerance of the twists and turns of a project born in COVID lock-down and on a rollercoaster ever since.

Finally, I am grateful to Chris and Hannah for many things, all the things – but on this occasion especially for every morning that you slept in long enough to give me headspace to write and for every evening that you put up with me falling asleep on the sofa long before (both of) you.

1   Introduction

This is a book about tools we use but that we have yet to learn to use well. Tools that we have become accustomed to and that are important to us, but that, it turns out, we know less about than we think: diversity and inclusion targets, or D&I targets. The aim of this book is to help us better understand and meaningfully use D&I targets. The book marshalls new knowledge and research to explain what D&I targets are, how we set them and how we work with them. D&I targets are useful for directing our thinking and attention. Used meaningfully they can drive change for better, and that is why we should plug our collective knowledge gaps and get proficient at using D&I targets and at having conversations about them.

This is also a book I hope we will not need for long. Our motivation for getting better at using D&I targets has to be that one day we will not need to use these tools anymore. That we will have built a UK screen industry – or any industry or sector, for that matter – where D&I targets are not a prominent feature anymore. It will take a while and quite a bit of work until we get to that point. But it is important to start this conversation by acknowledging that D&I targets are here *for now* but hopefully not *to stay*, like stabilisers for learning to ride a bike. For now, we have to work with targets and get better at doing that. But ultimately, we have to aim for a life without D&I targets. D&I targets are intended to address under-representation, exclusion and discrimination. In an ideal world, these problems would not exist and we would not need to use D&I targets to solve them. D&I targets are means, not ends – any other starting point would lead us on a journey of detours and cul-de-sacs.

Throughout the book, I often refer to 'we'. D&I targets, let alone diversity and inclusion, are a collective effort and endeavour, in the screen industries and elsewhere. And because – spoiler alert – there is far less research and evidence on D&I targets than I would like, it would feel particularly wrong to set up this book as a conversation between an all-knowing author authority and their hungry-to-learn readers. I wrote this book with a diverse (pun intended) community in mind: everyone who is part of the conversation about diversity

DOI: 10.4324/9781003434542-1

and inclusion, about equity, equal opportunity, fairness and social justice, in the screen industries and beyond.[1] I hope it will be useful especially for

- anyone who might be asked for explanations, evidence or advice regarding D&I targets because of their professional knowledge base – academics, researchers and industry experts;
- anyone who wants to or, for whatever reason, feels they should, use D&I targets – industry practitioners, policy makers, managers, organisational D&I leads;
- anyone who advocates for the under-represented groups that D&I targets are intended to benefit, who holds those who set D&I targets to account and who represents voices outside the mainstream of industry practice and knowledge creation.

The readership sketched in these three bullet points is a heterogeneous one, also because some of us will have the power to set D&I targets and others will not. It is certainly not a uniform and unified 'we'. I expect you all will, at some point, want to put clear blue water between what I write and your own take on D&I targets. Indeed, I hope for these reactions, as it is only through conversation and discussion that we will see any progress on diversity and inclusion. Against this background I am using 'we' throughout the conversation that is this book: based on the hopefully not too audacious assumption that you are here for the conversation and in the hope that the book's insights into D&I targets can support your part of the work, whatever that part may be.

Currently, D&I targets are mainly used as tools for (re-)allocating opportunity on the basis of people's characteristics such as gender, race or disability. When we stipulate how many per cent of group A should be in a larger group B we allocate opportunity – for education and training, for accessing a workplace or a particular role, for receiving promotion and better pay. Similarly, when we assess the diversity of speakers on a panel, judges on a jury or nominees for an award it is opportunity we are looking at: opportunity for voice, visibility, recognition or reputation. We use D&I targets to focus on opportunity because we have finally understood that the ways in which we have previously allocated opportunities produce deeply flawed and harmful outcomes. People with certain characteristics (white, not disabled, middle class) are much more likely to be given opportunities than people with other characteristics. To address such inequality and discrimination, we currently say to opportunity gatekeepers: 'When you decide on who gets opportunity, you have to aim to do it so that at least X% of the people who get opportunity come from group A and at least Y% come from group B'. We set so-called diversity targets[2] by stipulating how varied a group should look once we are done allocating opportunity.

While attention to diversity is progress, many problems remain with this approach, and I will briefly illustrate two. First, setting meaningful diversity targets is a lot harder than it looks, and we do not have much evidence of how to do it well. Diversity targets may seem intuitively plausible. For instance, there seems to be a certain logic to demanding that women make up 50% of whatever group we are looking at because women make up roughly one half of the general population. If we accept that logic for women and apply it to race, the proportion of Black, Asian and minoritised ethnic people in, say, a company's workforce would need to equal the proportion of Black, Asian and minoritised ethnic people in the population, right? At this point it already gets tricky: the race and ethnicity make-up of the United Kingdom varies hugely by region, and so does the location of different industries. So which reference point should we compare the diversity of a company's workforce to? Might regional demographic composition be a more appropriate reference point because the company operates in a regional labour market? What about a region in which class, poverty or living in rural versus urban locations influences the allocation of opportunity more strongly than race? Should companies in such a region set class targets alongside or instead of race targets? And once those questions are solved, how far off whichever reference point we have chosen does the diversity of a group need to be to warrant setting one or more diversity targets? Do we set the diversity target at the same level as the reference point? And what happens if the share of people with the characteristics we are looking at suddenly exceeds this benchmark – is that allowed? Do we drop the respective diversity target? And more fundamentally, how do we define the diversity characteristics we set targets for in the first place? What do our definitions make us see, what do they make us overlook?

Second, diversity as a focus and diversity targets as tools only deal with one slice of the overall issue we are looking at. Diversity is a measure of variation: it measures the extent to which units in a group or a footprint differ. Diversity helps us see variation, amongst people in a company's workforce, amongst the plant and animal species in a forest or amongst a tray of cupcakes. Diversity in itself is neither good nor bad; it is simply a measure to convey how varied something is. Diversity targets, when they are done well, can do a little more. If they take into account questions such as the ones outlined earlier, diversity targets can prompt change from a situation in which opportunity is always allocated to the same types to one in which a broader range of people get a chance to participate, have voice or visibility, earn reward or recognition. In that way, diversity as a neutral measure can be used for change for the better. There is much to be gained from using diversity targets in that way. But diversity and diversity targets by themselves only tell us who is there, who is visible, who earns how much. They do not carry information about people's experiences. For instance, being part of a group is not the same as not experiencing discrimination. A diversity perspective or target can capture who is and is not part of a group, but it cannot capture whether those who are in a group are experiencing discrimination or are feeling heard. Which means that a diversity target can even be met while people are still experiencing discrimination, harm and exclusion: interactions within a diverse group can still be shaped by ageist, sexist, racist or disablist views, for instance.[3] On their own, diversity targets can lead to people from under-represented groups being invited into a space in which others have not yet learned how to behave inclusively. Focusing solely on diversity and diversity targets has consequences that we need to be aware of. As I will set out in Chapter 5, if we only set diversity targets we are not just committing to giving more opportunities, we are also running the risk of working towards diversity at the cost of harming others, including the very people we want to give more opportunity to. Similarly, diversity as a measure does not tell us anything about what causes diversity or the lack of it: the processes that allocate opportunity, the structures that shape individual experiences, the perceptions that influence people's relationships. Processes, structures and perceptions are jigsaw pieces of the broader picture of inclusion. As a word, inclusion has become a common companion of diversity, from role titles such as D&I lead to companies' D&I strategies and D&I campaigns and events. Actual attention to inclusion – to processes, structures and perceptions, where they come from and what they result in – is less common and meaningful inclusion targets are even more rare. Current target setting still focuses squarely on diversity targets. The result is a lopsided approach in which we pursue the surface measures (diversity) rather than pay attention to the causes and dynamics (inclusion, or lack of it) of the thing we want to tend to (people's opportunities and experiences and our collective connections).

Returning to the language of tools, the first problem outlined earlier is one of using a tool correctly: how do we meaningfully design, implement and analyse with diversity targets? The second problem is one of using the right tool: which type of target should we set to improve diversity and inclusion? The next two chapters address these questions in reverse order. Chapter 2 spells out what D&I targets, diversity targets and inclusion targets are and what they focus on. Chapter 3 looks at using D&I targets, at the processes of setting them and working with them. Both chapters draw on examples from the UK screen industries but in ways that, I hope, easily translate into other creative industries and other sectors. Together these chapters provide us with a new framework and language for understanding D&I targets.

Chapter 4 applies our newly acquired framework and language to the UK screen industries. It describes how D&I targets are currently used, how industry practice is developing and which challenges of D&I target setting the UK screen industries are grappling with. This chapter is based on an analysis of 78 reports and documents published by broadcasters, funders and sector organisations. It paints the picture of a sector that has done pioneering work on D&I targets – both as a stock-take for the screen industries and as an inspiration for others.

In the final Chapter 5, I ask what is on the horizon for D&I targets, and diversity and inclusion work more broadly. This chapter deliberately goes beyond the initial evidence review and research to stimulate a deeper reflection on how D&I targets work – the foundations they rest on, the paradigms they adhere to and the thinking and doing that these foundations and paradigms enable or foreclose. There are critical questions about diversity and inclusion emerging right now, for instance, about the potential pitfalls of identifying and counting people to obtain diversity data, about how defining diversity characteristics can embed exclusionary ideas about identity or about how we can move towards more meaningful measures than representation. The final chapter points to some of these debates, to position the work that this book does and to point to where our thinking might develop.

The research underpinning this book was originally undertaken by myself and a research team as part of the *ScreenSkills D&I Targets Review*, which aimed to improve knowledge of D&I target setting. The review was commissioned to assist ScreenSkills' own practice but the outcomes proved so useful that ScreenSkills and the University of Glasgow decided to publish headline findings in an accessible format, as the *ScreenSkills D&I Targets Playbook* (ScreenSkills, 2023). Chapters 2–4 of this book follow up with more detailed evidence and arguments. The research we undertook found much less evidence and guidance than I had expected, certainly than I had hoped.[4] Where it was possible to plug those gaps on the basis of the newly undertaken research, both the *Playbook* and this book do so. In many cases though all that could rigorously be done was to point to what is still missing and to suggest how those gaps could be addressed. D&I targets, in the UK screen industries and elsewhere, are most definitely work in progress.

I hope that together these two publications can help us set and use D&I targets in a meaningful way – one that does not harm especially those of us who they are meant to support and that does not limit our imagination of who we could be, and become, as a society. Let's learn how to do D&I targets well so we can do without them – sooner rather than later.

Notes

1 A note on terminology: D&I targets are part of a much bigger conversation about equal opportunity, fairness, equality and equity, human rights, social justice, liberation, emancipation, decolonialisation, abolition and much more. These terms and conversations have long and complex histories and require space and attention that this book simply cannot offer. I have therefore decided to use the two terms used in the field from which the empirical research stems: diversity and inclusion (see Chapter 2 for definitions). The UK screen industries predominantly use those two terms even though equality, diversity and inclusion (EDI or DEI, for short) seem more common outwith screen.

2 I deliberately use the term 'diversity targets' here. Chapter 2 explains the difference between D&I targets, diversity targets and inclusion targets.

3 Diversity targets can, of course, also be met by organisations that cause physical, environment or sociocultural harms, for instance through their misuse of policing or border control powers, extractivist use of natural resources or spreading of

misinformation and hate speech. In other words, neither setting diversity targets nor achieving them certifies that an organisation is 'doing the right thing'.

4   To avoid misunderstandings: there are libraries full of research into diversity and inclusion, including a growing body of work on inclusion in the screen industries and cultural work more broadly. I am grateful to the many insightful researchers and writers in this area, from whom I have learned a lot. For this short book I have deliberately limited my references to work (a) that focuses on the narrow topic of D&I targets as the industry practice common in the screen industries (e.g. which terms they use and why, how they are set, how they are worked with, what the challenges, unintended consequences and remaining knowledge gaps are) or (b) that speaks directly to specific aspects of the D&I target setting practice we observe in the UK screen industries. My perspective on the literature has been driven by the empirical phenomenon I had been tasked with looking at. And it is that specific phenomenon for which we do not have much evidence and research. For the specific topic of D&I targets, we have, despite repeated efforts, not been able to identify much recent work that goes beyond gender diversity on company boards – a related issue, of course, but not quite at the heart of what we are trying to understand here.

2 D&I targets
Definitions & rationales

This chapter lays the conceptual foundations for thinking through D&I targets. It defines what D&I targets are and describes the most common types of D&I targets. It explains how and why to distinguish between (a) D&I targets, D&I data collection, monitoring and reporting, and quotas; (b) diversity targets and inclusion targets; and (c) internal and transorganisational D&I targets. The chapter considers the diversity characteristics that D&I targets might be set for and concludes by discussing how intersectionality can be factored into D&I target setting.

2.1 What D&I targets are *not*

It may be counterintuitive to start this chapter with a discussion of what we are *not* talking about when we talk about D&I targets. But in my experience working with industry and academia, people come to the conversation about D&I targets not with a blank canvass. Instead, everyone comes with more or less vague images of what they have encountered before. Some of these images are more helpful than others. In an attempt to achieve as clear a picture of D&I targets as possible, this section therefore discusses two concepts related to D&I targets: D&I data collection, monitoring and reporting, and quotas. These two concepts populate many of the not-blank-anymore canvasses that we bring to the D&I target conversation and have a habit of getting in the way of understanding D&I targets on their own terms. My hope is that talking about D&I data collection, monitoring and reporting as well as quotas first can clear the view on D&I targets, what they are and how they work, and insulate the D&I targets conversation against the most common misunderstandings.

Both in and beyond the UK screen industries it has become standard for companies and organisations to collect, monitor and report data related to diversity and inclusion. Typically, these efforts focus on collecting data about individuals, aggregating this data and monitoring it over time. The reports analysed in our research showcased such diversity data reporting at the level of individual organisations (e.g. BBC, 2021a; Channel 4, 2019a).

DOI: 10.4324/9781003434542-2

Examples of cross-industry reporting include Ofcom (2021a) and CDN (2022) and – beyond the screen industries – Arts Council England (2021b) and Creative Scotland (2022), who publish regular summary reports of diversity data submitted by organisations as a condition of licencing or funding. At the time of writing, Diamond (CDN, 2023) is the only tool that collects and publishes industry-level data directly from individuals on an ongoing basis. Other data sources are developing more regular cross-industry, direct reporting mechanisms as well, for instance Ukie's (2022) *Games Industry Census*, UK Screen Alliance's (2019) *Inclusion and Diversity in UK Visual Effects, Animation and Post-Production* survey and, outwith screen, the Publishers Association's (2022) survey of publishing employees and UK Music's (2022) *Workforce Diversity Survey*. ScreenSkills (2023) collects data directly from participants in its training and skills programmes but does not yet publish regularly from this data. Such analyses and reporting of diversity data often also involve comparisons with reference data. Frequently cited reference data for workforce diversity are population or labour force statistics, which we will discuss in Section 3.3.

To some degree collecting, monitoring and reporting D&I data is mandatory, either generally or as a condition for accessing funding or being considered for awards. For instance, since 2017 UK organisations with 250 or more employees have been required to report gender pay gap data (Government Equalities Office, 2023a), and there are calls to extend this obligation to pay gap data for race and disability (HM Government, 2021). In the screen industries, the UK communications regulator Ofcom has made licencing conditional on the provision of workforce diversity data for gender, race and disability as well as general information about D&I interventions (Ofcom, 2020a). Similarly, the BFI (2019) and BAFTA (2020) require the submission of D&I information with funding applications or to demonstrate eligibility for awards. Last not least, production companies need D&I data to demonstrate how they comply with broadcasters' commissioning targets (e.g. BBC, 2018a; ITV, 2018).

Data collection, monitoring and reporting are considerable undertakings in their own right. They are also indispensable for D&I target setting, for three reasons. First, they provide baseline data (see Section 3.2). D&I data describes the starting point that is considered for target setting and, in combination with the reference data, enables us to formulate a D&I target in the first place. Second, data collection, monitoring and reporting are the vehicles through which we chart progress towards a D&I target. Data points collected over time allow us to check in on whether actions towards targets are yielding results and to course-correct if needed. Third, as activities, data collection, monitoring and reporting raise important questions about the methods with which we want to undertake them. Their purpose – to provide insight into D&I-relevant aspects of our organisational set-up, outputs and engagement – forces us to consider how that insight can be achieved, that is, which data can best convey the insights we require, and how that data can be obtained in ways that are reliable, credible, transparent and coherent as well as ethical and legal (e.g. Bryman, 2016; D'Ignazio and Klein, 2020). D&I data collection, monitoring and reporting that is robust and reliable as well as practical and sustainable in its organisational context is a serious undertaking in itself. And in addition to methodological and practical quandaries, also has implications for how we understand and perceive diversity and inclusion – a question we will discuss in Chapter 5.

All that said, and fully acknowledging the – intellectual, financial and micro-political – efforts that go into good-quality data collection, monitoring and reporting, it is important to distinguish this whole area of D&I theory and practice from D&I target setting. D&I target setting builds on D&I data collection, monitoring and reporting but goes an important step further. Where organisations set D&I targets of whatever type (see Section 2.5), they commit to actively working towards improving diversity and inclusion and to affecting change that is reflected in the measures chosen. A D&I target is a commitment towards action. A D&I target does not just describe an aspired state of affairs for, for example, workforce diversity, financial investment or inclusive culture. Taken seriously, a D&I target implies the commitment to bring that state into being. This action-based aspect distinguishes D&I target setting from collecting, monitoring and reporting D&I data.

D&I targets and D&I data reporting are often presented in similar formats, using percentage figures and reference data such as population or labour force statistics. Data reporting can therefore look similar to a target statement because of the data points and sources cited. In addition, such reporting can be understood as implying that it is the reference data point which should be achieved, that is, comparisons can be read as targets.

Visuals and syntax also play a role with the second related concept, that of D&I targets: quotas. In the D&I context, the term quota is used to refer to a compulsory minimum share of people with a particular characteristic in a group, for example, a minimum quota of disabled people for senior management or for care-experienced participants on a training. Quotas have a 'share of something' format, often expressed as percentages. In the screen industries, most D&I targets currently also have that 'share of something' format and are expressed in percentages. Because of this overlap, we often hear 'D&I target' and think 'quotas', and jump to conclusions about diversity targets and under-representation that are, as Chapter 5 will discuss, limiting, unhelpful and ineffective. On the other hand, this distinction is also important, because D&I targets as we define them in Section 2.2 are, in principle, lawful, whereas in the United Kingdom, the use of compulsory quotas as a D&I tool is generally not allowed. The UK's 2010 Equality Act makes important distinctions between positive discrimination, which is unlawful, and positive action, which is lawful for specific cases and under very limited conditions and should not be considered without specialist legal advice

(Government Equalities Office, 2023b). Somewhat unhelpfully given the context of English language web searches, UK legislation in this area differs from legislation around D&I quotas and affirmative action in the United States.

Of course, D&I targets, quotas and the collection, monitoring and reporting of diversity data all exist in the same thought universe. And there are important overlaps – for instance, we need diversity data to work with D&I targets. But they play different roles in the conversation about diversity and inclusion, and to properly understand what D&I targets are and can be we need to keep these distinctions in mind, in theory and in practice.

2.2   What D&I targets are

To understand D&I targets, we first need to define three terms: diversity, inclusion and targets. Especially for diversity, there are now libraries worth of definitions available in research and policy literature, let alone popular media and airport shop management books. To be frank, these definitions vary greatly in their transferability and coherence – important criteria used for defining the quality of concepts in academic work (e.g. Bryman, 2016) – and therefore in their usefulness. Vernā Myers' by now ubiquitous quote 'diversity is being invited to the party, inclusion is being asked to dance' (Myers, 2014), for instance, is not entirely unhelpful. It points, in a relatable if slightly crude way, to a fundamental truth of D&I work: just getting a diverse group of people together is not 'job done'. Similarly, it is of course not wrong to say that diversity 'refers to seeking the equal or greater representation of underrepresented, historically marginalised people' (Tulshyan, 2022: 6). But for understanding D&I targets, we need more precise definitions that help us identify what we are and are not looking at.

Diversity is a measure of variation within a specified population at a particular point in/over a stretch of time. It tells us how many different expressions of a characteristic are present in that population and how prominent each expression is. To apply a diversity-lens, we need to define which characteristic we are interested in (e.g. religion or belief) and which different expressions of that characteristic we recognise. For instance, for the characteristic 'religion or belief', we might recognise individuals describing themselves as atheist, Buddhist, Christian, Confucian, Jewish, Muslim, Sikh etc. Using these expressions of the characteristic religion or belief, we can then establish the diversity of a population with absolute figures or percentages, for example, saying that X number of individuals described themselves atheist, Buddhist, Christian etc. or that a group was made up of X% of expression A, Y% of expression B, Z% of expression C (for a helpfully in-depth reflection on the term diversity, see Risberg et al., 2019).[1]

Inclusion is best understood as a perspective that examines the degree to which practices, structures, relationships, provisions, allocations, communications etc.

are experienced as open, participative, connecting, empathic, respectful of difference and equitably designed. Inclusion asks after the effects of our actions and inactions, and after the experiences our processes and structures bring into being for everyone that interacts with them. A basic example is recruitment: how do we define the role that needs filling and the person who we deem appointable? Who do we reach out to and how? How openly do we explain the appointments process and how well trained are the staff involved in spotting exclusionary practice? Notably, these questions can only be answered for the recruitment process in question: even if we are satisfied that one recruitment process was conducted in an inclusive manner, there is no guarantee that the next process will be inclusive, too. We will need to ask the same questions again. Inclusion is both 'in the making' and in the remaking. It is not just to be found (or not) in our thinking and doing, it is constantly re-thought and re-done (or not).

Both diversity and inclusion need to be operationalised to set D&I targets. We need to define how, in a particular context, we want to make diversity or inclusion visible, what 'counts as' diverse or inclusive. Drawing extensively on the research undertaken for the *D&I ScreenSkills Review*, the remainder of this chapter explains how diversity and inclusion are operationalised as targets. Targets describe an explicit intended result, a state to be achieved at a particular point in time and the ways in which achievement towards target will be monitored (e.g. Grote, 2017; Reeves et al., 2018).

Building on these definitions, we define a diversity and inclusion target (D&I target) as follows:

- an explicitly stated, timebound and measurable outcome;
- that relates to diversity and inclusion; and
- that is to be achieved through strategic and/or operational action.

A D&I target is therefore not just any ideal state we would like to see achieved, but a commitment to achieve a specific outcome that is brought about by action and for which achievement towards target can be monitored in a specified way.

In principle, D&I targets can relate to any aspect deemed relevant to the D&I problem at hand. Based on the research and evidence analysed, we should distinguish between diversity targets and inclusion targets – which the following sections will explain in more detail.

2.3   Diversity targets

Our academic, industry and policy conversations overwhelmingly focus on one specific type of D&I targets: *diversity targets*. Diversity targets are targets that relate to the representation of different characteristics and that quantify what that representation should look like. Diversity targets typically measure representation as the percentage of people with a specific characteristic within a bigger group, for instance in a company's workforce or amongst participants of a training programme. Where that percentage is deemed to be too low or at risk of being too low, a diversity target is then set for the minimum percentage of people with a specific characteristic within a bigger group, for example, the share of employees from Black, Asian and minoritised ethnic groups. A diversity target can state a representation figure to be achieved at a particular point in time (e.g. X% by year Z), or for a particular moment or activity, for example, a film funding application or training programme. Instead of giving an overall representation target, diversity targets can also stipulate the increase in representation, for instance, an X% annual increase of staff with characteristic Y, or an X% increase of participants with characteristic Y from one training programme to the next.

The diversity targets discussed in the general equality, diversity and inclusion literature tend to be *workforce diversity targets*, that is, targets for the share of workers with characteristic X in the workforce (for overviews, see Noon and Ogbonna, 2021). More nuanced approaches suggest setting diversity targets for specific stages in the employment cycle or for different hierarchy levels. For example, workforce diversity targets might stipulate that X% of new recruits should come from certain socio-economic backgrounds, or that X% of senior managers should identify as disabled. Diversity targets can be set for specific points in the employee lifecycle, such as recruitment, retention, progression and promotion, and companies outwith the screen industries are increasingly doing so (BITC, 2020). For instance, BITC's (2020) study found that nearly one in two (46%) companies were setting targets for ethnic diversity at board and executive levels. Targets at different hierarchical levels can be useful for increasing 'the overall talent pipeline' (Workplace Gender Equality Agency, 2013: 14).

In the UK screen industries, the use of diversity targets has spread beyond workforces. Recognising the industries' output and business model, diversity targets in UK screen are commonly also set for on-screen output and training interventions:

- *On-screen diversity targets* relate to the representation of individuals with different characteristics on screen. Examples might be the share of Black, Asian or minoritised ethnic characters in a drama, or the age profile of characters a player meets in a computer game.
- *Participant diversity targets* relate to the representation of individuals with different characteristics amongst the participants of a training programme or intervention, whether general or D&I focused. Participant diversity targets typically stipulate the minimum share of participants on a training programme or intervention that should come from a particular group, for instance, that live outside London or that have caring responsibilities.

Provided they use good-quality data (see Section 3.7), representation measures can convey important information about the diversity of a group. For instance, diversity measures can be highly effective for evidencing the scale of under-representation in an area. Moreover, diversity targets work with quantitative data that, once obtained, is comparatively easy to manage, analyse and report using standard business software like MS Excel. Qualitative data, for example, text answers from staff surveys, requires more specialist knowledge and time to analyse and manage effectively.

But it is important to remember that representation measures are not designed to provide insight into workers' experiences. Diversity as a lens does not tell us whether people feel valued at work or whether they are remunerated equitably (see Section 4.6). We need to bear these methodological limitations of diversity targets in mind when designing an organisation's D&I targets approach. But where people with specific characteristics are persistently under-represented in a group, setting diversity targets can provide effective levers for improving diversity and inclusion overall – which makes setting diversity targets for workforces, on-screen representation and training programmes well worth the effort.

2.4 Inclusion targets

Our research found a range of targets that went beyond diversity and representation and related to various aspects of inclusion such as individual experiences or organisational processes. These *inclusion targets* used broader indicators of inclusive practice that reported on, for instance, financial D&I investments, on-screen narratives or how comfortable people felt expressing their identities. Our research suggests that the following types of inclusion targets are most relevant for the UK screen industries:

1. *Pay gap targets*: Pay gap targets state an organisation's ambitions for closing differences in earnings by a particular characteristic. In the United Kingdom, public reporting of gender pay gap data is mandatory for companies with more than 250 employees. Differences in earnings can indicate a lack of equal opportunity, for instance, that staff with a particular characteristic do not as easily access better paid positions as other staff. Screen industries organisations are increasingly using pay data to also set targets for closing pay gaps. Pay gaps are most commonly considered for gender, race or disability but could also be set for class and parenthood (Wreyford et al., 2021).
2. *On-screen portrayal targets*: On-screen portrayal targets relate to the output produced; for instance, the gender identities gamers can choose for an avatar, the age profiles of the main and supporting actors in a drama or how characters with specific characteristics are portrayed on screen. On-screen portrayal is a more holistic perspective than on-screen representation: on-screen portrayal is the result of editorial decisions not just about

who is included, but how they feature and what narratives are told by and about them (e.g. Saha, 2010).

3. *Intervention targets*: Intervention targets can be set to formalise an organisation's intention to undertake certain types of D&I interventions. For instance, a company might set the target to run annual mentoring programmes or diversity trainings, or to set up staff fora. Or a company may decide to set targets for increasing its disclosure rates for diversity data (e.g. BITC, 2020). While intervention targets are mentioned in the literature as being used in industry, they are not systematically labelled and discussed as a distinct type of D&I targets.

4. *Investment targets*: Investment targets stipulate a D&I-related monetary investment, either as an absolute figure or as a percentage of an organisation's budget. Our research did not find evidence on investment targets, for instance, on how investments might best be calculated. Nevertheless, in the UK screen industries, investment targets are slowly beginning to emerge, for instance, as a budget to be spent commissioning content that foregrounds otherwise under-represented characters and narratives, or content produced by individuals from under-represented groups (BBC, n.d.).[2]

Indicators for inclusion targets can be quantitative or qualitative. Quantitative inclusion targets might, for instance, state an intended investment budget or an aim to halve the disability pay gap or double disclosure figures for religion. Especially for intervention targets or on-screen portrayal, qualitative indicators can be more appropriate, for instance, narrative evidence of inclusive recruitment practices or an analysis of individuals' reports about feeling included and supported at work.

2.5   D&I targets

At the time of writing, inclusion targets are only just emerging in the UK screen industries – and elsewhere. In the research and evidence reviewed, D&I targets were so strongly understood to be diversity targets that other target types were not systematically discussed. Inclusion targets were mentioned (though not called that) in stakeholder documents for the UK screen industries, but there was no general or academic discussion of their intended use or of how they should be designed or applied. While diversity targets in the sense and format with which they are described in Section 2.3 were recognised, presented and discussed as diversity targets, the conversation about inclusion targets is still finding its feet. Recent general research on D&I targets such as Noon and Ogbonna's (2021) study mentions inclusion but shows the idea of targets to be applied only to workforce diversity.

A key aim of this book is to provide a framework and language for D&I targets, in the UK screen industries and beyond. The research undertaken for the *ScreenSkills D&I Targets Review* and updated for this book suggests that our framework needs to

- distinguish between diversity targets and inclusion targets;
- distinguish, within diversity targets, between workforce diversity targets, on-screen diversity targets and participant diversity targets; and
- distinguish, within inclusion targets, pay gap targets, on-screen portrayal targets, intervention targets and investment targets.

As D&I target setting practice develops, other types of diversity targets or inclusion targets might emerge. Similarly, in other industries other target types might be relevant alongside or instead (some of) these target types. Distinguishing between diversity targets on the one hand and inclusion targets on the other, and between the different types of targets within these two big categories, will enable us to be more precise in our conversation about D&I target setting – is it diversity that we are aiming to improve, or inclusion more broadly? It will also enable us to be more strategic and effective in our interventions. For instance, if we want to improve inclusion more broadly, diversity targets will only tell us so much about our progress towards that aim. Chapter 5 will discuss these points in more detail.

Figure 2.1 summarises the framework of D&I targets at the heart of this book. This framework, and the definitions of diversity and inclusion targets that underpin it, was built bottom-up, analysing and systematising current practice in the UK screen industries. The definitions and most target types, however, easily translate to other industry contexts. Workforce and participant diversity targets or intervention and investment targets are – or can be – used in, say, banking, construction or education just as well as in the screen industries. On-screen representation and on-screen portrayal are the only

D&I targets in the UK screen industries

Figure 2.1 Types of D&I targets in the UK screen industries

genuinely screen-industries-specific target types in the framework. However, on-screen targets can easily have equivalents in many other industries – from the portrayal of characters in school books and print adverts to how we think about and represent, for instance, citizens, patients and consumers in areas as different as town planning, health care and product design. The framework suggested in this book should therefore be helpful not only for the screen industries but also well beyond them.

2.6   Internal versus transorganisational D&I targets

D&I targets are typically set by a company or an organisation for itself. For instance, a training organisation might decide to recruit or promote a higher share of employees from previously under-represented groups. Based on our *ScreenSkills D&I Target Review* research I will refer to these targets as *internal D&I targets*. Internal targets refer to a D&I issue that an organisation wants to act on for itself. They are not internal in the sense that they need only relate to what happens inside an organisation – say the organisations' workforce or promotion processes. Internal D&I targets can, and often do, refer to how an organisation engages with its environment. A broadcaster ring-fencing budget to commission work that fulfils stretch targets for on-screen portrayal, for instance, would be an internal D&I target that engages beyond the organisation. But such a target would still be internal in that it would be set by the organisation for itself.

Internal D&I targets are widely used in the UK screen industries, most prominently to increase workforce diversity but also to improve inclusion more widely (see Chapter 4 for more details). However, in these industries, D&I targets are also set by organisations for other organisations. Common examples are targets attached to TV commissioning or funding. Broadcasters and funders such as the BFI set D&I targets that production companies have to fulfil. For example, ITV set on-screen representation targets for women (50%), people of colour (15%), disability (8%), and gender identity (7%) (ITV, 2019). Similarly, when commissioning training interventions, ScreenSkills sets D&I targets for the mix of participants on a training and the training providers contracted to deliver the training need to fulfil these participant diversity targets (ScreenSkills, 2023). The BFI's Diversity Standards set other organisations an inclusion target for interventions: 'Your project is offering training opportunities . . . to people from under-represented groups' (BFI, 2019: 5).

Our review of research and evidence showed that it is important to understand D&I targets set by one organisation for another organisation as a thing in itself. Drawing on my previous research about work and production in the cultural economy (Eikhof, 2014), we named these targets *transorganisational D&I targets*: targets that do not always apply to the whole screen industry but that do transcend one organisation and affect at least one other organisation.

Transorganisational D&I targets have an important dynamic: the organisation setting a target is not in control of the actions delivering on the target, and – depending on whether targets are unilaterally set or mutually negotiated and agreed – the organisation delivering on the target is not, or at least not wholly, in control of target setting. This scenario has implications for effective D&I target setting. As we will discuss in Section 3.1, targets need to be ambitious as well as achievable to be effective. Setting an ambitious yet achievable D&I target for another organisation requires insight into that organisation to understand which actions are and are not possible. But how can such insight best be achieved? How can, for instance, a London-based commissioning broadcaster best know whether a workforce diversity target is or is not ambitious yet achievable for a production company in York?

Evidence on transorganisational D&I target setting is extremely limited. We have not found a systematic distinction of internal and transorganisational D&I targets in the literature, or a discussion of the dynamics that require attention to make transorganisational targets work. Where appropriate, the following chapters will draw on evidence for internal D&I targets to discuss transorganisational D&I targets. And for readability, I will only distinguish between internal and transorganisational D&I targets where differences in the substance of internal and transorganisational targets and target setting make that distinction necessary. But despite the lack of evidence on transorganisational targets, what research there is suggests that recognising the difference between internal and transorganisational targets and building better knowledge about them is essential for working with D&I targets in the UK screen industries and beyond.

2.7 Diversity characteristics

At the core of the conversation about D&I in work and employment is the idea that experiences of work, access to opportunity in work, or outcomes from work should not be systematically impacted by individual characteristics that are not directly related to the work itself. Bracketing discussions about the social construction of merit (see Chapter 5), the consensus is that differences in experiences, opportunity or reward are acceptable if they are based on differences in effort, skills or outputs, but not if they are based on, for instance, skin colour, belief or gender identity. We use D&I targets as a tool to make this foundational idea of diversity and inclusion reality.

In the D&I conversation, individual characteristics that are relevant to experiences of inclusion and exclusion, discrimination, opportunity, advancement and outcomes are commonly referred to as diversity characteristics. Which individual characteristics we set D&I targets for depends on the context we are looking at and the aspects of diversity and inclusion we would like to address. In the UK screen industries, D&I targets are most often set for gender and race/ethnicity, followed by disability and sexual orientation, as well as, increasingly, socio-economic background (see Section 4.3). However, our research found no explicit guidance on how an organisation might want to choose which diversity characteristics to set targets for. Legislation and political and academic debate likely influence which diversity characteristics attention is directed towards in both data collection and target setting. But there is no research or evidence that explicitly demonstrates this point, let alone suggests evidence-based rationales for choosing diversity characteristics to set targets for. Similarly, at the time of writing there seems to be no guidance on how to define and operationalise targets for specific diversity characteristics, for example, which ethnicity/race characteristics targets might be set for.

Looking at the collection of diversity data rather than D&I target setting more specifically in the United Kingdom, the nine characteristics protected through the 2010 Equality Act – age, disability, gender reassignment, being married or in a civil partnership, being pregnant or on maternity leave, race, religion or belief, sex, sexual orientation – seem to be influential. PwC (n.d.), for instance, finds that in the United Kingdom, data on sex/gender, age, ethnicity, sexual orientation, gender identity and disability are 'typically collected'. Data 'increasingly' collected according to PwC (n.d.) include socio-economic background (or 'social mobility'),[3] faith, caring responsibilities as well as more detailed disability information (e.g. type of condition/impairment, neurodiversity). Similarly, a small-scale survey of 269 mostly private sector organisations found that data on gender, age, race/ethnicity, disability, religion and belief and LGBTQ+ (listed in the order of prevalence) was collected by 60% or more companies (Carty, 2020). Information on caring responsibilities and social mobility (not further defined) was collected much less frequently, by 16% and 13% of companies, respectively (ibid.). Notably, these studies though report what is happening rather than the reasons for it, that is, for choosing to focus on some diversity characteristics and not others.

2.8   D&I targets and intersectionality

The term intersectionality was coined to draw attention to the fact that characteristics such as sex/gender, age and race can combine to amplify the disadvantages and exclusion an individual experiences (Crenshaw, 1989, originally focusing on Black women). A disabled worker with caring responsibilities, for instance, might face much higher challenges accessing a labour market beyond their immediate region than someone who either is not disabled or does not have caring responsibilities. Intersectional approaches can help identify cases in which improved opportunities in one regard (e.g. better gender equality) may still leave individuals disadvantaged because of other characteristics relevant to inclusion (e.g. their race) (CIPD, 2018). In the above example, accessible transport might improve the disabled workers' regional reach but caring responsibilities might limit how they can exercise that mobility beyond, say, school hours. For the creative industries generally, Carey et al. (2020: 2) find that intersectionality creates a 'double disadvantage', for instance, when class interacts with other factors – such as gender, ethnicity, disability and skill levels. Which is why, as interviewees in a study of Canadian TV pointed out, a shadowing programme for women directors for instance is only effective at supporting women's careers if it is also paid and does not leave participants with '"the extra expense" of financing time spent shadowing' (Coles and Eikhof, 2021: 13).

Intersectional analysis, however, requires both specific data and models; it goes beyond merely reporting representation data for more than one diversity characteristic. Intersectional analysis of diversity data and in particular how identity characteristics intersect with the material conditions of establishing and maintaining a career is under-developed both in the screen industries and generally. CIPD's (2018) evidence review of diversity management argues that although 'researching intersectionality is a complex task . . . inclusion research should be more inclusive and appreciate individuals' multiple identities both in research and practice' (CIPD, 2018: 25). In the UK screen industries, too, most research focuses on singular diversity characteristics (Ozimek, 2020) and 'intersectionalities are not systematically explored' (CAMEo, 2018: 40). Industry also recognises the lack of an intersectional perspective. Ofcom (2020a: 34), for instance, emphasises the importance – and lack of – intersectional analysis and urges broadcasters 'to provide data, where possible, on the representation in their workforce of intersecting characteristics'. The regulator argues for gaining a better understanding specifically of how class and ethnic background intersect to affect workforce representation (Ofcom, 2020b). The Creative Industries Council's review and analysis echo this assessment for the UK's creative economy as whole (CIC, 2020; CIC, forthcoming).

But while rigorous quantitative intersectional data and models may not (yet) be available, evidence on the workings of intersectionality generally suggests two possible approaches for addressing intersectionality through D&I targets:

- *Setting targets for interventions that remove cross-cutting barriers*: Cross-cutting barriers are obstacles to workforce participation and advancement that individuals from more than one under-represented group find disproportionately difficult to overcome (CAMEo, 2018). For instance, recruiting through personal networks disadvantages individuals from working-class backgrounds who tend to have less access to 'the right' networks as well as women who are able to access the networks but whose professional credits are perceived differently in networking situations that those of men (CAMEo, 2018). Similarly, long and anti-social working hours are problematic for workers with particular conditions and impairments as well as for workers with caring responsibilities. Removing such cross-cutting barriers and implementing inclusive practices will be especially effective in improving opportunities for individuals with intersecting diversity characteristics. In the examples above, formalising recruitment practices could be particularly beneficial for working-class women, and offering job shares could especially improve opportunity for disabled carers. D&I targets for interventions that change industry practice in ways that remove cross-cutting barriers could therefore be effective for addressing intersectional exclusion.

- *Setting intersectional participation targets:* Participant diversity targets stipulate the share of individuals with particular characteristics amongst all training participants (see Section 3.2). Such targets can be set to require participants on general trainings or D&I interventions to belong to more than one under-represented group. Interventions with intersectional participant diversity targets could be tailored to a particular set of intersecting characteristics and address the challenges resulting from the particular intersection – an example would be a career progression programme for Black women. Intersectional participation targets could also ring-fence general skills development programmes for participants who belong to more than one under-represented group (e.g. technical trainings or training to become a mentor for participants who are disabled and come from specific socio-economic backgrounds). Importantly, intersectional target setting needs to take into account potential conflicts between targets. Demographical variations with respect to race, for instance, can make it necessary to adjust target levels.

Developing methods and evidence for intersectional disadvantages is an important task, and one that both industry and academia should tackle together (e.g. CAMEo, 2018; Carey et al., 2020; CIC, 2020). But the above suggestions show that we do not have to wait while that work is being undertaken. The current evidence is insightful enough for us to include intersectional perspectives in the design of both diversity targets and inclusion targets.

Notes

1 Behind this technical definition of term diversity lie, as Sara Ahmed (2007) demonstrates, strategic uses of the term, for instance, to avoid terms like equity or to conceal 'histories of struggle for equality' (ibid: 235).
2 Cultural industries organisations like the BBC and Arts Council England have, for some time, used targets for investment by region. It should be noted though that these targets are not necessarily D&I targets: targeting cultural production in a region does not automatically translate into regional diversity in the workforce involved. Investment-related inclusion targets would relate to investments made with the primary purpose of increasing diversity and inclusion amongst the screen industries workforce.
3 Throughout the literature, various terms are used to refer to individuals' socio-economic background (class, socio-economic background, social mobility), often without further definition. In the United Kingdom, the main measure is the National Statistics Socio-economic classification (NS-SEC) (ONS, n.d.), which focuses on occupation.

3 D&I target setting

Steps & processes

This chapter digs into the process of setting D&I targets. It outlines key steps of setting targets and introduces principles of good D&I target setting. The chapter then discusses which baseline data to use for understanding the status quo and which reference data to compare that status quo to. It explains how to set D&I target levels and target ranges. The chapter finishes with thoughts on setting timelines, monitoring progress towards targets and reviewing D&I targets.

3.1 Setting D&I targets

Our research set out to understand what was needed to use D&I targets meaningfully and effectively. A key finding was that, across academia, industry and policy, we need to find a unifying language, a framework for talking about D&I targets in the first place, for asking better questions so we could get to more precise answers. The previous Chapter 2 has done one part of that language job: it has brought evidence of what is already happening in the UK screen industries in conversation with what little research there is to offer new definitions and a framework. This chapter continues the language-finding, defining task but focuses more on the processes of working with D&I targets. To 'do D&I targets well' we need to know not just what D&I targets are, but also have a shared language for what surrounds them – not only, but probably most importantly, for the baseline and reference data that D&I targets work with.

To develop the definitions for this part of the D&I target language and framework, we need to cast our net wide. There exists a substantive body of research especially on gender targets, including internationally comparative reviews of where soft targets versus binding quotas are set and large-scale quantitative analysis of correlations between quota legislation and the presence of women on boards (for overviews and summary studies, see, e.g. Denis, 2022; Jaishiv, 2022; Kang et al., 2023; Mensi-Klarbach et al., 2021; Oldford, 2022; Viviers et al., 2022). But there still is little dedicated research into processes of D&I target setting or information about existing D&I targets setting practice (see Noon and Ogbonna's (2021) case study for a rare example). Many companies

DOI: 10.4324/9781003434542-3

do, of course, publish their D&I targets, and Chapter 4 will discuss in more detail what those D&I targets are in the UK screen industries. But two important limitations need bearing in mind for this chapter. First, what little research and practice we have access to strongly focuses on diversity targets and, in particular, workforce diversity targets. We know much less about all the other types of targets introduced in Chapter 2, in particular about inclusion targets. Second, most of our current evidence concerns the targets themselves, not the underpinning rationales for which targets to set and for how to set them. Where we have knowledge about what is being done, we do not necessarily know how or why.

The general, and generally implicit, idea is that D&I target setting consists of four basic steps:

- Step 1: identify the current situation using baseline data (Section 3.2).
- Step 2: compare baseline data to reference data (Section 3.3).
- Step 3: set a target and target level (Section 3.5).
- Step: 4: monitor achievement towards target (Section 3.6).

While our research found no explicit guidance on how this basic four-step process should be executed, some aspects of target setting were mentioned frequently enough in research and industry publications to understand them as principles of good target setting: targets should be aspirational, achievable, action-based, clearly formulated and identify accountability. The penultimate principle in that list is a generic one that echoes common general principles of target setting in business (e.g. Grote, 2017; Reeves et al., 2018): D&I targets should clearly state their purpose, the evidence based used to set them and the mechanisms for monitoring achievement towards targets (Workplace Gender Equality Agency, 2013). The other principles, however, warrant a little further exploration.

First, in what little evidence there is, the most prominently mentioned requirement for D&I targets relates to ambition and achievability: targets should be ambitious (synonymously: aspirational, stretching) as well as achievable (synonymously: realistic, meaningful). The need for targets to be ambitious was not further discussed; it probably stems from a general notion that easily achievable targets would not spur action for change. The argument for achievability however was explicitly made. According to the Workplace Gender Equality Agency, for instance, 'overly ambitious' targets are less likely to be accomplished and can 'reduce the motivation to change' (2013: 9). Vinnicombe et al'.s (2020) study of women's representation at board level concludes that 'setting stretching but realistic targets is considered industry best practice' (p. 30, similarly Kang et al., 2023). The 2017 McGregor-Smith Review into racial inequalities also argues for targets that are 'challenging, [but] reflect the reality of the situation' (p. 13; see also CIPD, 2019; Menzies, 2018; Seramount, 2017, see also Box 3.1). The BBC's (2021b) Diversity & Inclusion Plan also aims for 'targets that are stretching but achievable' (p. 11). But while achievability was clearly recognised as an important principle of D&I target setting, there was little guidance on how achievability might be established. For internal workforce diversity target setting, the Workplace Gender Equality Agency (2013) recommends a company level review of workforce composition that includes size as well as anticipated job changes and turnover. Similarly, the BBC (2021b) advocates a (not further specified) use of 'predictive analysis' to inform achievable targets. However, these suggestions merely state which data to consider. They do not recommend how that data might be interpreted to assess a potential D&I target as achievable or not. They also seem to understand achievability as mainly relating to the size of the gap between baseline data (the status quo) and reference data (where an organisation might want to be). Such a view would be myopic: whether targets are or are not perceived as achievable will depend not only on the size and shape of a gap but also on whether target recipients see themselves as in control of actions that can close the gap. For instance, an organisation that operates in a racially diverse labour market may think it quite achievable to close even a big gap between their current race profile and that of the labour market if the main change that is required is a different recruitment process. By contrast, an organisation in a less racially diverse labour market might see closing even a small gap between its workforce profile and the labour market profile as not very achievable.

Second, good target setting recognises the link between targets and actions. Chapter 2 established that D&I targets are commitments to actions, and it is this link to actions that distinguishes targets from collecting, monitoring and reporting diversity data. Evolving evidence on processes of target setting echoes these thoughts: D&I targets should be related to actions that those tasked with delivering on the targets are in control of (McGregor-Smith Review, 2017; Workplace Gender Equality Agency, 2013). PwC, for example, attributes the rise of its intake of graduates from Black, Asian and minoritised ethnic groups to 39%, from a baseline of 23% and against a target of 30%, to changes in recruitment practices such as removing UCAS scores from graduate entry requirements and engagement with a wider group of schools and universities (McGregor-Smith Review, 2017).

Third, D&I targets need to create accountability. For targets to be effective, it needs to be clear who is accountable for delivering on them, especially at the level of individual managers or leaders. The McGregor-Smith Review (2017) recommends including D&I objectives in the annual appraisal of all leadership roles. Channel 4 went a step further and made the achievement of diversity targets part of the annual variable pay for their senior managers and editorial staff (Channel 4, 2015). On the one hand, creating such accountability can signal that D&I targets are taken seriously. On the other hand, and probably more importantly, accountability makes D&I targets more effective: targets are more likely to be met when their achievement is made a key performance indicator (Workplace Gender Equality Agency, 2013). In transorganisational D&I target setting, equivalent principles are applied when, for instance, funding or commissions are made dependent on the achievement of D&I targets.

In themselves, these three aspects of D&I target setting feel somewhat commonsensical. However, our research raises an empirical and a conceptual point. Empirically, our analysis of screen industry reports and publications found little if any information on target setting processes (see Chapter 4) and therefore on any underlying principles, rationale or criteria. To be clear: the *Review* did not find that principles of good target setting were not or are not being adhered to in the UK screen industries. The research merely allowed us to note the absence of information and that it was therefore not possible to say whether or not principles of good target setting had been applied.

This empirical point is important in its own right: in the spirit of transparency and accountability, it would be good practice to publish information about how D&I targets were set. The absence of such information is particularly noteworthy though in connection with the conceptual point: the above principles are markedly less straightforward to apply when setting transorganisational D&I targets. There is no dedicated research, evidence or guidance specifically about how one organisation should set a D&I target that another organisation is responsible for delivering. Assessing what evidence there is through the lens of transorganisational relationships, two aspects stand out.

First, if one organisation sets D&I targets for one or more other organisations, there will be an increased need for clarity regarding terminology and rationales. Transorganisational D&I targets will need to be accompanied by definitions of key terms (e.g. for diversity characteristics, regions, interventions) to avoid misunderstandings about the parameters under which change is to be delivered. Transorganisational D&I targets should also be accompanied by a clearly stated rationale for the target, including why it was chosen and how it was set. This information is essential if D&I targets are to be meaningful to target recipients – and thus effective tools for change.

Second, for transorganisational D&I targets the combination of the 'ambitious but achievable' principle, the action-based aspect of targets and the need for target recipients to be in control of delivery on targets becomes a potential Bermuda triangle of good D&I intentions. Setting an ambitious yet achievable D&I target for another organisation requires considerable insight into the other organisation's actions and circumstances. For organisation A to set a target that organisation B perceives as ambitious yet achievable – and that is therefore a functioning, effective target – organisation A will require good insight into which actions are and are not possible for organisation B. There will likely be a multitude of aspects that shape whether and how such vital insight into another organisation's abilities and limits can be gained. For instance, if organisation B's opportunity to access funding from organisation A depends on fulfilling D&I targets, B might have an incentive to overstate its ability to deliver on D&I. The nature and quality of the relationship between a target setting organisation and a target receiving organisation will therefore have significant impact on how effectively transorganisational targets can be set.

Box 3.1   Ambition versus achievability in D&I target setting

The **Welsh Government** (2021) set ambitious targets for both the external recruitment and the promotion of *disabled people*. Against a baseline of 6% of disabled people working in the organisation in 2020, it strived to achieve a target for externally recruiting 20% of people who identify as disabled by 2026 and 30% by 2030, with targets and actions being reviewed against achievements and lessons learned by 2026. The Welsh Government also aimed to promote disabled people beyond the level that matches their population share (22.7% in Wales). It argued that 'meeting these very ambitious targets will be extremely challenging and will be dependent on continued focus and investment. However, we would prefer to have stretching targets that we will struggle to achieve than to lack ambition on this very important issue'. (ibid.: 9)

3.2   Baseline measures for D&I targets

When we set a D&I target, we – more or less explicitly – acknowledge that we are not happy with the status quo and that we want to change it. To assess the status quo, and to then come to the conclusion that we need to set a D&I target, we require baseline measures: good-quality data that informs us about a D&I-relevant aspect of the current situation (c.f. CIPD, 2019; McGregor-Smith Review, 2017). What that baseline data relates to entirely depends on the D&I issue we decide to examine. Baseline data might, for instance, be information about the current participant diversity of training interventions, the diversity of a company's workforce, current pay gaps or evidence of current investment in D&I interventions. However, in the same way that D&I targets can cover any D&I issue deemed relevant but most D&I targets currently in use are diversity targets, current research and evidence squarely focus on baseline measures for diversity targets, and more specifically, workforce diversity targets.

Baseline measures for diversity targets typically use diversity data: data about individuals' characteristics, for example, their sex/gender, age, race/ethnicity etc., that is deemed relevant to diversity and inclusion. Such diversity data is gathered about an overall group of people (e.g. a company's workforce) and compared to reference data (see Section 3.3) to identify under-representation of individuals with a particular characteristic.

Diversity data is typically obtained by asking individuals to confidentially and voluntarily fill in monitoring forms, often via a company HR system (see also Box 3.2). This data needs to be managed and processed in line with legal requirements (e.g. the UK Data Protection Act 2018 (Gov.uk, 2023) or EU

General Data Protection Regulation (GDPR EU, 2023)). Where diversity data is published, even within an organisation, individuals' personal information needs to be protected and data needs to be processed in ways that do not allow identifying individuals. This consideration is particularly important where both the sample for which data is reported and the percentage of individuals with a particular characteristic are small (e.g. if in a department of 10 employees 1% identify as LGBTQ).

In the screen industries, diversity data is gathered both organisationally and transorganisationally.

- *Organisational diversity data* is gathered by employers, in particular the main broadcasters. Their data is published in organisational reports (e.g. BBC, 2018b; Channel 4, 2018; ITV, 2020; Sky, 2021) and in summary accounts such as those by Ofcom (2020b).
- *Transorganisational diversity data* is collected and published in several ways, most prominently through Diamond (e.g. CDN, 2021) and the BFI Diversity Standards (e.g. BFI, 2020). ScreenSkills and Pact also collect diversity data for training participants via monitoring forms (e.g. Screen-Skills, 2019). Diversity data that transcends organisations is also collected through infrequent surveys such as Ukie's *Games Industry Census* (Taylor, 2022) or the UK Screen Alliance's (2019) *Inclusion and Diversity in UK Visual Effects, Animation and Post-Production* Survey. Secondary analysis of general data sources such as the ONS Labour Force Survey (e.g. Carey et al., 2021) provides additional information about the D&I profile of the screen industry workforce.

As with many aspects of D&I target setting, our research unearthed no evidence or guidance beyond diversity targets. To a degree, however, understanding which information could usefully serve as baseline data is not the most complicated question: to understand D&I investment, resource measures relating to staff time or monetary investment will likely be appropriate, and for pay gap targets various data points for staff remuneration will be needed. Assessing the status quo for employee experience or, in the screen industries, on-screen portrayal will require slightly different methods that work with qualitative data (e.g. surveys, content analysis), but here too, sensible starting points should not be out of reach. The Creative Industries Councils' *Charting Progress Framework* (CIC, forthcoming), for instance, suggests which aspects about D&I interventions organisations might capture to set inclusion targets for interventions or investment – for example, empirical footprint or frequency of an intervention or investment. Notwithstanding some more fundamental questions about working with D&I data (see Chapter 5) and the need to build better evidence on which data to use in D&I target setting generally (e.g. ScreenSkills, 2023), standard business methods for gathering data about organisational processes and practices should yield reasonably robust baseline data for most D&I targets. The standard methodological principles for working with data pertain here too: baseline measures need to be reliable (i.e. they need to produce stable measures of a variable) and valid (i.e. credibly measure what they say they measure) (Bryman, 2016). The more challenging question is how this baseline data should be interpreted and translated into target levels. The following Sections 3.3–3.5 on reference data and setting D&I target levels explore potential answers.

Box 3.2   Disclosure rates

The percentage of individuals who have provided information on a diversity characteristic is known as the disclosure rate. PwC's (n.d.-a) *Diversity data guide* advises to aim for a disclosure rate between at least 60% to ideally 80%. However, both in the screen industries and generally, low disclosure rates are a 'major problem' (CIPD, 2019) – partly because individuals are not motivated to provide their data and partly because individuals are unsure who can access their data and how it might be used (see also Chapter 5).

Engaging employees on how the data is being used can 'significantly improve response rates on an ongoing basis' (PwC, n.d., see also McGregor-Smith Review, 2017). Trust and an inclusive culture are also linked with higher disclosure rates (CIPD, 2019). Where the disclosure rate is low, PwC's (n.d.) *Diversity data guide* suggests gathering additional qualitative data for further insight.

Targeted campaigns can improve disclosure rates for diversity data. At Lloyds Banking Group, for instance, regular communication campaigns sponsored by senior leadership and supported by guidance information for managers led to a 4% increase in self-disclosed ethnicity data on the HR system (McGregor-Smith Review, 2017). In the screen industries, Channel 4's internal 'This Is Me' campaign which featured videos about the working day of disabled staff achieved even more dramatic results. In the wake of 'This Is Me', 90% of employees updated their diversity data and disability disclosure almost quadrupled from 3% to 11.5% (Channel 4, 2019b).

3.3   Reference data for D&I targets

Baseline measures provide information about a current situation. This information is then compared to reference data: data that provides information on the same D&I issue in a different context. The previous section remarked that choosing baseline measures is not the most complicated question. Choosing reference data requires a bit more reflection. The reference data we are most used to seeing in D&I target setting and – crucially – in diversity data reporting is demographic data for a nation's workforce or population. Section 3.4 will discuss using this type of reference data. First though we need to take a step back and reflect more broadly on what reference data is meant to do and therefore, what we need to bear in mind when choosing which reference data to work with.

More often than not, my conversations with industry and policy follow a well-trodden pattern: I mention 'diversity and inclusion' and the person I am in conversation with tells me how their staff or student body compares to demographic indicators for the United Kingdom. In the introduction, I already hinted at the limitations of such a focus on diversity and I will expand on these thoughts in Chapter 5. I briefly want to pick them up here though to break this reflex that links mentions of D&I to demographic data as 'the' reference point.

In principle, reference data can be any data that we identify as useful for comparing or benchmarking our own status quo with. When we work with reference data, we are in the business of comparing ourselves to what is happening elsewhere. For those comparisons, the first question has to be how we can know about the issue that interest us for our own context – our company, our industry – in a different context. If we have decided to use workforce diversity data to understand whether workers with specific characteristics find it more difficult to get work in our company than elsewhere, comparing our staff profile to demographic data elsewhere can make sense. If our question is, however, how active our company is in addressing issues of diversity and inclusion, benchmarking ourselves to fellow employers in our industry might not yield much information. Organisations in the same context tend to broadly mirror how they do business. We might find ourselves to be running more D&I interventions than our competitors or to be investing more D&I budget. But if our industry performs poorly on D&I overall, such a benchmarking outcome might merely mean we are doing better than a bad average – not necessarily a reason to be cheerful.

Our research found little evidence or guidance on which reference data to use for inclusion targets. Some organisations reported benchmarking themselves against data from other organisations in and outwith the screen industries. The BBC, for instance, benchmarks the socio-economic diversity of its workforce against public sector organisations and KPMG (BBC, 2018c). Ofcom, for its own workforce, points towards diversity indicators such as the Stonewall Workplace Equality Index or the Social Mobility Foundation's Social Mobility Index (Ofcom, 2018a). In principle, benchmarking can be a potentially useful exercise for developing inclusion targets. However, as flagged earlier, it requires reflection on which benchmarks are appropriate to use and why. For instance, for a large broadcaster looking to close pay gaps, non-broadcasting organisations of a similar size and staff/job structure might be a more meaningful benchmark than other broadcasters of a much smaller size. How useful benchmarking can be will also depend on the information other organisations or industries make available. If a D&I target is to pertain to staff experience, for instance, finding out how included staff feel elsewhere might not easily be possible, either because other organisations do not gather that type of data or because they might not publish it, for instance for reputational reasons.

At the time of writing, the evidence base for choosing reference data and working with it is still thin. It is therefore difficult to say what – beyond building better evidence – we should exactly be doing. As with baseline measures, to some extent we can turn towards general methodological principles: we want our reference data to be reliable and valid (see Section 2.1). However, the availability of reference data is less in our control than the availability of baseline data. We thus need to reflect on what we can usefully compare our baseline measures to and what good-quality data is available to us from elsewhere. If we cannot identify useful reference data, we may need to revisit the baseline measures we want to use. Beyond these points, the only honest option for the moment is to acknowledge that good practice regarding reference data for D&I targets is work in progress, and to share our workings and reflections as openly as possible, so that we can collectively build better evidence of 'what good looks like'.

3.4 Using demographic data as reference data

By far the most visible reference data in the UK screen industries takes the form of demographical statistics. Such statistics tell us what variations of individual characteristics (e.g. age, disability or sex/gender) we might find in a group, and how common different versions of each characteristic are in that group. In statistical terms, an individual characteristic is a variable (e.g. age) with different values (e.g. 15 years and under, 16–24 years, 25–34 years, 35–49 years, 50–64 years, 65 and over, as used in the 2021 Census (ONS, 2023b)). The distribution for this variable shows us the number or share of people with a particular characteristic (e.g. the number or percentage of people in each age group).

Such statistics feature mainly in relation to workforce diversity (e.g. Davies Review, 2011; Parker Review, 2017). The three most commonly used statistical measures are population, working-age population and labour force:

- *Population*: This reference group is the broadest possible one. It includes the entire population of a geographical footprint, typically a nation or country. The population includes everyone residing in that footprint, not just individuals currently in work or of working age.

  Population data shows the representation of different groups undistorted by any issues of entering or remaining in the labour market. Where barriers to work or to looking for work exist, for instance for disabled people or carers, population data gives a better idea of how these groups are represented overall than labour force data. However, population data also includes individuals who cannot yet enter the labour market because they are too young and individuals who have permanently retired from paid work.

- *Working-age population*: The working-age population comprises all individuals aged 16 to 64 within a geographical footprint, typically a nation or country (e.g. ONS Labour Force Survey).

The working-age population is the pool from which the labour force can be drawn. Like population statistics, working-age population statistics provide information about the representation of different groups generally; they are not skewed by potentially unequal opportunities of actually entering the labour force (see later).

The working-age population excludes, however, a small but significant group of individuals still working at age 65 and over (around 10% of that age group). This exclusion can be relevant for D&I targets relating to the protected characteristics age and disability.

- *Labour force*: The labour force comprises 'the proportion of a country's working-age population that engages actively in the labour market, either by working or looking for work' (ILO, not dated). It excludes anyone who might want to work but is not officially registered as looking for work. The labour force will be significantly smaller than the working-age population if many individuals of working age face significant barriers to remaining in work or to looking for work. Such barriers might, for instance, be a country's welfare system making it difficult to register as job seeking.

Data on these three reference groups can be drawn from multiple sources. In the United Kingdom, the main sources of population data come from the Office for National Statistics (ONS): the Census (ONS, 2023b) (if reasonably up to date) or the Annual Population Survey (ONS, 2023a). Data on working-age population or labour force participation primarily comes from the ONS' Labour Force Survey (ONS, 2023c). The Census aims to gather data on every individual resident in the United Kingdom once in a decade. The Annual Population Survey (APS) and the Labour Force Survey (LFS) run much more frequently (every three months) but cover only a sample of fewer than 400,000 individuals in the UK population. All three sources contain information on the majority of diversity characteristics and can be broken down to national and regional level. Access to some formats of Census, APS and LFS data requires specialist registration and statistical skills.

According to the Creative Equity Toolkit (n.d.) website, national population statistics are commonly used as reference data for identifying under-representation and setting D&I workforce diversity targets. For the UK screen industries, information about which reference data is used is often ambiguous; for instance, publications appeared to use population and working-age population synonymously when stating D&I targets. However, the following example of Diamond provides a useful illustration of working with different reference data sources depending on the diversity aspect in question.

Diamond collects data on the diversity characteristics of contributors to broadcast content (e.g. CDN, 2021). It records data on six characteristics (gender, gender identity, age, race and ethnicity, sexual orientation, disability) and reports on workforce diversity and on-screen diversity. Diamond uses different reference data sources for the analysis of off-screen workforce diversity and on-screen diversity:

- For workforce diversity in off-screen roles, Diamond uses labour force statistics first, and population figures only where labour force statistics are unavailable, for example, population estimates for different ethnic groups (CDN, 2021). The use of labour force statistics as reference data allows Diamond to compare access to the broadcasting labour market with access to the UK labour market more broadly. The implicit assumption is that if that comparison shows the broadcasting workforce to be less diverse than the national labour force, there might be broadcasting-specific barriers to labour market participation and advancement in play that need addressing.
- For on-screen diversity Diamond uses population statistics as reference data. On-screen diversity as a D&I measure is based on the assumption that diverse TV audiences should see themselves reflected in on-screen content. As on-screen content is viewed by everyone, not just those of working age or in work, Diamond choses population data as the most relevant reference data (CDN, 2021). This logic of comparing audience data with population data is quite common. Another example of referring to population data in this way is Arts Council England's (2021a) aim for targets to ensure organisations' activities 'reflect the communities in which they work' (pp. 52–53).

Importantly, Diamond itself only reports diversity data for UK broadcasting. It does not set D&I targets. CDN's Doubling Disability initiative (CAMEo, 2019) used Diamond data to set transorganisational disability targets for the Diamond broadcasters. However, the above example is only illustrative of how reference data sources are used in reporting data, not in setting targets.

Our evidence review did not find much evidence or guidance using reference data to set participant diversity targets. The BFI and ScreenSkills are positive examples in that they state which data source they use. The BFI (n.d.) indicates that it used working-age population data to set diversity targets that apply across its funding recipients, including BFI NETWORK. ScreenSkills (2019) cites UK Census data on disability, ethnicity and gender as its reference data sources. In both cases, however, the actual target levels set are not a like-for-like match to UK working-age population or population statistics and it is not obvious how exactly ONS population statistics were translated into actual D&I targets.

For some D&I questions, screen-industries-specific data sources can provide useful reference data. Appendix 2 provides an overview of four sources: Diamond, Ofcom's summary reports of broadcaster-reported employee data and two screen-industries-specific data sources compiled by UK Screen Alliance and Ukie. The latter three data sources are not regular data collections. While they can provide useful touchpoints for D&I data setting, their use will be more limited than that of regularly updated data sources. Screen-industries-specific data sources can be helpful in target setting, for instance to evidence the under-representation of a particular group. Similarly, data from these sources might be used to gauge the likely gap between the representation of a particular group within the UK population and in the UK screen industries. Data from these sources should be used cautiously though: using representation levels from screen-industries-specific data as target levels would risk reproducing existing problems with under-representation in the screen industries workforce and likely not drive change.

3.5   Setting D&I target levels

The most glaring gap in the evidence on D&I target setting concerns the actual setting of targets: which D&I target type(s) to choose, which diversity characteristics to set targets for and which level to set a target at. Our research found very little information on how these decisions are currently made or guidance on how they should be made. Some publications contained implicit rationales that we could piece together reading across documents and between the lines. For instance, a D&I report might declare an overall intention of having its workforce or output 'better reflect the UK's population', and a later chapter might then mention D&I targets with levels that very broadly mirror the representation of different groups within the UK population. But we did not find concrete explanations on how baseline measures and reference data had been used to identify and set targets and target levels. Especially workforce diversity targets have become so established in the UK screen industries that industry publications and conversations seem to imply some underlying established practice. But we soon come across, as ScreenSkills CEO Seetha Kumar put it, 'questions about detail, consistency and good practice guidance' (ScreenSkills, 2023: 8). We thus have to start this section, too, with the recognition that good practice on choosing targets and target levels is work in progress and more experience and evidence will be needed before we know 'what good looks like'.

At least for workforce and participant diversity targets – and, it should be stressed, only for these two target types – there is enough evidence to discuss a few aspects of identifying target levels. First, there seems to be an emerging recognition that the principle of achievability needs to be taken into account when setting diversity target levels. A concrete example in the UK screen industries is that of Doubling Disability, a CDN-led intervention that committed the UK's main broadcasters to doubling the share of disabled people in off-screen broadcasting roles between 2018 and 2021 (CDN, n.d.). At the time of target setting, only 4.5% of broadcasting workers in off-screen roles identified as disabled, compared to 17% of the UK's working-age population. Faced with such a considerable difference and mindful that D&I targets need to be realistic (see Section 3.1), CDN explicitly opted to not set a target level that mirrored working-age population statistics, but one that was deemed more achievable (9%).

Second, and also related to achievability, there is some discussion of local or regional adjustments to diversity target levels for race/ethnicity. The share of Black, Asian and other minoritised groups in the population, working-age population and labour force varies across the UK nations and English regions. The McGregor-Smith Review (2017), for example, states:

> Some of the best examples we have seen of targets being delivered have come from employers who tailor these to local circumstances, allowing regional business managers to take ownership. For instance, where employers are based in areas of low BME density, expecting them to reach 14% of their workforce is unrealistic. However, this works both ways and where employers are located in urban areas with high BME populations such as London, Birmingham or Manchester, aiming for 14% would be neither representative nor ambitious enough. For a national organisation, I would expect to see overall targets of 14%, rising to 20% by 2050 in line with predictions for UK population growth and composition.
>
> (ibid., p. 14).

According to BITC's (2020) survey, only about a third of employers use 'national and local demographic data to set targets/KPIs for recruitment to ensure the applications received are reflective of the talent pool' (BITC, 2020: 28). In the UK screen industries, the BFI aims for 40% for those identifying as ethnically diverse in London and 30% for those identifying as ethnically diverse outside London (BFI, n.d.).

Regional variations are only considered for race and ethnicity though, and often for the – rather broad – comparison of London/South East England versus the rest of the United Kingdom. There is no discussion, let alone detailed guidance, on how to take into account production hubs outside London, for instance, in Glasgow, Manchester-Salford, Leeds, Cardiff and Bristol (CAMEo, 2018; Ozimek, 2020), where the race and ethnicity profile of the (working age) population and labour force vary in comparison to the UK population average as well as to population averages of the respective greater region. Our research also found no guidance on how regions should be defined and where regional reference data should be drawn from. The principle of achievability would suggest that where reference data shows regional variation, workforce and participant diversity targets should be adjusted using regional reference data rather than UK-wider reference data. Such regional adjustments will likely be especially important in transorganisational target setting, for instance, to avoid a UK-wide operating organisation setting targets that locally delivering organisations find too difficult to achieve.

Third, the single-figure percentage format used in diversity targets has instigated an interesting, though not yet very prominent conversation about target ranges. The European Institute for Gender Equality (2018, see also Coles et al., 2018) suggests aiming for gender balance rather than a 50/50 split between women and men. Gender balance is defined as having no less than 40% women or men in the group in question. If we consider the idea of target ranges in combination with the principles of good target setting (Section 3.1), target ranges turn out to have considerable advantages, especially for transorganisational diversity target setting:

- Target ranges are more likely to be seen as meaningful: in practice, data collection and reliability alone make it unlikely that a diversity target expressed as percentage figure can be deemed to be 'exactly' met. For instance, there are typically sizeable gaps in diversity data because not all training participants or staff fill in diversity monitoring forms or return a high share of 'prefer not to say' answers. Under those circumstances, calculating whether the share of people with a specific characteristic does reach a target of, say, 14% or maybe remains just below that figure can be both methodologically challenging and feel somewhat arbitrary, if not outright meaningless. Setting a target range instead of a single-figure target signals understanding of the conditions under which an organisation is trying to achieve the target, and thus makes the target more meaningful and relevant – and thus more likely to meet the principles of good target setting and to be more effective.
- Targets set as strict percentages can incentivise practices that are, ultimately, counterproductive for achieving inclusion. A percentage figure target for workforce diversity can act as an incentive to make what has become known as 'diversity hires': appointments that informally prioritise someone's diversity characteristics so that diversity targets are fulfilled. Diversity hires carry a significant danger of stigma: appointees are seen as hired not for their skills, talent and experience, but for their identity. In a society that sees itself as meritocratic, such perceptions are not compliments. Hiring for diversity can thus harm the individual and will likely also not lead to meaningfully inclusive cultures overall (e.g. Maxwell, 2004; Saha, 2010).
- Target ranges can provide flexibility in target achievement for shorter interventions or interventions with a small group of participants. Participant

diversity on a one-day seminar, for instance, might be lower than the diversity of a target population despite inclusive organisation and marketing. A target range, ideally applied to a series of seminars, would likely be more meaningful and appropriate. Similarly, an 8% workforce diversity target for LGBTQ+ for a project team of 15 people is mathematically impossible to achieve.

Overall, target ranges can help prevent a counterproductive preoccupation with 'counting diversity' and free up attention and resource for more meaningfully improving inclusion. Target ranges are thus more likely to complement the principles of good target setting (see Section 3.1). Building on the 'gender balance' concept, target ranges could be set so that the lower end of the target range equates to 0.8 × reference data value and the upper end equates to 1.2 × reference data value. That means, a 50/50 diversity target for gender would become a 40%–60% target and an 18% target for disability would, if rounded, become a 14%–22% target.

Beyond these discussion points, substantive questions remain: How big would the gap between baseline and reference data need to be to trigger the setting of a target? At what point can a target count as fulfilled and be dropped, and what might the political ramifications of dropping a target be? Chapter 5 returns to these questions and how we might approach target setting despite the current gaps in evidence.

3.6   Setting timelines and monitoring progress

To work effectively D&I targets need to be timebound: they need to clearly indicate by when a target is to be achieved. Because, as emphasised in Chapter 2, targets are commitments to action, timelines for target achievement need to take into account how long it will take to execute the action that the target commits to and whether there might be any additional time required for the action to show measurable results. Effective timelines will thus differ from target to target. Diversity targets for recruitment or for non-executive board members, for instance, may be quicker to achieve than diversity targets for internal promotion. Similarly, it might not take long to meet a D&I investment target but much longer to establish the aspired suite of D&I interventions that this D&I investment makes possible.

Where improving diversity and inclusion requires complex organisational change, timelines of around five years tend to be recommended (e.g. Workplace Gender Equality Agency, 2013), for instance, in recent UK reviews on gender and race/ethnicity diversity at board level (Davies Review, 2011; Parker Review, 2017). Large organisations may decide to set targets around a five- to ten-year period to allow for broad-scope action plans to be implemented and changes to occur.

However, as emphasised by the principles of target setting (see Section 3.1), D&I targets also need to be perceived as concrete enough to require present-day action. Where targets are set with mid- to long-term timelines, it is good practice to monitor progress on a regular basis, using the measures agreed in target setting (Workplace Gender Equality Agency, 2013), on either a six-monthly or annual basis over this period. The McGregor-Smith Review (2017) into racial inequalities, for instance, recommends setting five-year aspirational targets for organisations and monitoring progress against targets annually.

Finally, we need to consider data collection when we set timelines for D&I targets. Monitoring progress against D&I targets is likely to be less resource intensive for numerical targets. Data on workforce diversity, training participation or pay gaps is relatively easy to collect and analyse, and thus lends itself to shorter monitoring cycles. Data on, for instance, interventions or – in the screen industries – on on-screen portrayal is more resource intensive to collect and also require a meaningful number of incidents to report on (e.g. D&I interventions to have been delivered) (see CIC, forthcoming). We need to consider such practicalities and resource requirements for data collection so that timelines for monitoring and target achievement do not compromise principles such as meaningfulness. In particular, the time and resources required for data collection need to be proportionate to the time and resources of delivering D&I interventions. As a rule of thumb, shorter monitoring cycles for D&I targets are more likely to be appropriate for numerical measures and longer monitoring cycles for D&I targets with non-numerical measures.

3.7   Reviewing D&I targets

As with many other aspects of D&I targets, there is no guidance on reviewing D&I targets. In the absence of better evidence, a fruitful approach seems to be to periodically check whether the D&I targets set continue to comply with the principles for target setting: Do the targets remain clear, action-based, ambitious and achievable, and the arrangements for monitoring and accountability appropriate? If not, how would the portfolio of targets need to be revised to reflect the principles of good target setting? At the level of the individual target, a review will likely consider how the target is defined and whether the target level is appropriate, or should be increased or lowered.

For setting review cycles or timelines, the action-based principle of target setting will be important to bear in mind: Review cycles need to allow actions towards target achievement to yield results. Another consideration might be the availability of updated reference data. Reference data such as working-age population statistics is available in shorter cycles than recommended for D&I target setting overall, so should not be too much of a constraint. But where reference data comes from more smaller or more industry-specific sources (e.g.

Section 3.3), their publication cycles can be useful to take into account. In the UK screen industries, another consideration could be to align D&I target review cycles with those of leading industry organisations, especially those that regularly set targets for other organisations (e.g. BFI, main broadcasters). However, the stakeholder consultation undertaken as part of the *ScreenSkills D&I Targets Review* did not return any information on how frequently these stakeholders review their D&I targets.

Where D&I targets have been set with short- to mid-term timelines of around five years, it seems reasonable to undertake target reviews towards the end of that timeline. Where progress monitoring indicates target achievement well ahead of schedule, an earlier review and adjustment could be considered (see Box 3.3). For D&I targets with longer timelines of between five and ten years, it seems reasonable to review targets at least at the halfway point to establish if they still comply with the principles of good target setting.

Finally, where D&I targets are set and delivered upon transorganisationally, any meaningful target review would need to involve conversations between the organisation(s) setting the targets and the organisation(s) delivering on the targets.

Box 3.3 Adjusting workforce diversity targets

Channel 4's overall diversity targets set in 2015 for 2020 aimed to match 'national representation'. The targets were to increase in representation of staff from Black, Asian and minoritised backgrounds from 15% to 20%; achieve a gender split of 50:50 women/men; and increase the share of disabled staff from 1.9% to 6% and of staff identifying as LGBT+ from 2.4% to 6% (Channel 4, 2015). Some of these targets were revised ahead of schedule in 2019, with the race & ethnicity target extended to 2023 and the doubling of the disability target by 2023. In both cases, the actual representation in 2018 was already quite close to the target (Channel 4, 2019a).

---

4 D&I targets in the UK screen industries

This chapter explains how D&I targets are currently used in the UK screen industries. Based on in-depth analyses of 78 publicly available publications from broadcasters and sector organisations, it reviews cross-cutting trends, details what diversity targets are typically set for and at which levels and discusses the use of reference data. The chapter then outlines the emerging use of inclusion targets and, to close, challenges of D&I target setting in the UK screen industries.

4.1 A D&I ecology perspective

D&I targets are not new to the UK screen industries. There is now, in the early 2020s, enough work and experience with D&I targets for us to analyse and comment on. The research underlying this book did exactly that, and its overall finding – 'we need to better understand D&I targets and how we use them meaningfully' – is the reason this book exists. But to get better at meaningfully using D&I targets, we need to know our starting point. Not just so that we can chart progress, but also so that we can anticipate where barriers to improvement might show up and where we can draw on existing strengths.

This chapter uses the findings from the *ScreenSkills D&I Targets Review* to paint a more detailed picture of D&I target setting in the UK screen industries. It is based on the analysis of 78 reports and D&I documents published 2010-2023 on the websites of key screen industries organisations: BBC, BFI, CDN, Channel 4, ITV, Netflix, Ofcom, Pact, Sky and ViacomCBS. The *ScreenSkills D&I Targets Review* looked at which types of targets were set in these documents and how they were justified, which diversity characteristics targets were set for, how baseline data and reference data were used and how D&I target setting was discussed (see Appendix 1 for details).

The *Review* found clear patterns in how D&I targets are used across UK screen. This result in itself is not surprising: the UK screen industries are dominated by a fairly small group of key organisations. Broadcasters, funders and sector organisations publicly talk about what they do and are in conversation

DOI: 10.4324/9781003434542-4

and exchange with each other through shared platforms such as CDN and Creative Industries Council, D&I-focused industry events and trade press coverage. The broadcasters are subject to the same Ofcom regulation and D&I-related licence conditions, and as employers they need to adhere to the same D&I-related legislation (e.g. 2010 Equality Act, Gender Pay Gap legislation). Key D&I personnel frequently move between broadcasters and sector organisations. Under such conditions, we would expect a certain degree of isomorphism amongst organisational practices (e.g. Alvarez et al., 2005; Boxenbaum and Jonsson, 2017), and indeed, previous research has found strong similarities in, for instance, how gender inequality is understood (e.g. Eikhof et al., 2019).

These patterns, this degree of isomorphism, justify us talking about the UK screen industries as a collective, or a D&I ecology. They justify using phrases like 'typically ...' or 'most prominently ...' to describe industry practice rather than having to report on each organisations' individual actions. The degree of isomorphism also justifies commenting on the context of the UK screen industries' D&I ecology. And it allows pointing out gaps or shortcomings in what the collective of organisations in this ecology does. This ecology perspective is conceptually appropriate for capturing the transorganisational nature of screen production generally, and D&I target setting specifically. Transorganisational D&I targets, that is, targets set by one organisation for another (see Section 2.6), are a key feature of the UK screen industries. It would therefore be neither academically rigorous nor practically helpful to look at D&I targets as something screen organisations do in isolation. But it is important to understand that this understanding of the screen industries as a collective or ecology also means that what each individual organisation does by way of D&I target setting, for better or worse, somewhat disappears out of view and blends into the overall picture. The findings reported in this chapter should therefore not be read as an endorsement of any one organisation's D&I target setting practices or a critique of another's. They should be read as describing the status quo of the D&I ecology that the organisations whose publications were analysed form together.

4.2   The bigger picture

Before getting into the detailed findings, this section provides an overview of D&I targets within the screen industries' D&I ecology. From this perspective, five findings from the *ScreenSkills D&I Targets Review* are important scene setters. First, D&I targets are key pieces of the D&I jigsaw, but they do not dominate the picture. D&I targets are part of a wider effort to improve diversity and inclusion. The documents analysed showed an established and continuously evolving conversation about D&I interventions, D&I data, motivations for improving diversity and inclusion, and barriers to improvement (see also CAMEo, 2018; Carey et al., 2020; CIC, 2020; Ozimek, 2020). Diversity and inclusion have clearly become an area of collective practice into which the UK screen industries invest time, effort and financial resource, and about which there is a public debate within and outwith the industry, for instance, about the diversity of BAFTA nominations and awards (e.g. Abdul, 2023; Katsha, 2023). D&I targets are embedded within screen industry practice and conversations but they are not the focus.

Second, the monitoring of D& data remains more prominent than D&I target setting. The organisations whose publications we analysed use D&I targets more and more explicitly. However, it remains important to distinguish between the collection, monitoring and reporting of D&I-related data and the commitment to concrete D&I targets. The former is widely established. At organisational level, the broadcasters publish regular reports about the make-up of their workforces (e.g. BBC, 2021a; Channel 4, 2019a; ITV, 2018; Sky, 2021b; Viacom/Channel 5, 2016). Across the industry, Diamond, Ofcom, ScreenSkills, UK Screen Alliance and Ukie generate and provide transorganisational diversity data, which in turn feeds into the data work undertaken in individual organisations. D&I targets as defined in Section 2.2, that is, as explicitly stated, timebound and measurable outcomes that relate to D&I and are to be achieved through strategic and operational action, are much rarer and thus less visible. In addition, where D&I targets are set in the UK screen industries, they tend to be diversity targets expressed as percentages and thus look similar to diversity data monitoring, which works with the same formats. As a consequence, it is easy not only to overlook proper D&I targets in the UK screen industries, but also to misinterpret the ubiquity of data reporting as widespread D&I target setting practice.

Third, the imbalance between diversity data monitoring and D&I target setting is mirrored and somewhat amplified by a skewed data focus. As much as the collection, monitoring and reporting of data related to diversity and inclusion have become industry standard, our research found them squarely focused on workforce diversity and on-screen diversity, and, to a lesser extent, pay gaps. Data on D&I interventions, on-screen portrayal and D&I investment was not systematically published and appeared to be much less comprehensively collected. These patterns in data collection and publication are important because they reinforce the lopsided attention to diversity over inclusion as a concept and diversity targets over inclusion targets as tools – an imbalance that, as we will discuss in Chapter 5, is ultimately counterproductive to meaningfully improving diversity and inclusion.

Fourthly, D&I targets are still something the UK screen industries do rather than discuss. There was – at the time of writing this book, and indeed the reason for writing it – no visible conversation about, or reflection on, D&I target setting. Overwhelmingly public information about D&I targets was limited to statements of D&I targets. These statements were not accompanied by explanations of how a target had been set or which (other) targets – by type or by diversity characteristic – had been considered. Even references towards actions that were expected to affect progress towards target achievement, that is, statements about how the respective target would work, were scarce. There were no signs of established collective conversations about rationales for target setting or about target setting processes. The overall appearance of D&I targets in the documents was a slightly paradoxical one: D&I targets seemed somewhat naturally part of the picture, alongside statements about overall D&I aspirations and descriptions of concrete interventions, but the mechanics of how they were imagined to work as part of the overall D&I effort were not really explained.

Fifthly and finally, at the time of the research, D&I target setting in the screen industries was notably more nuanced and developed than in other UK sectors. Outwith the screen industries D&I targets overwhelmingly focused on workforce diversity (e.g. Noon and Ogbonna, 2021). By contrast the UK screen industries clearly recognised that in addition to their workforce reflecting the diversity of the UK's overall workforce, their screen outputs also needed to reflect the diversity of their audiences, that is, of the whole UK population. This recognition may now be growing in other, in particular creative, industries (see CIC, 2020; and, for a longer standing concern, Arts Council England, 2021b). The screen industries' business model and products might make questions about whether audiences see themselves in what they see on screen more likely to be asked and possibly also easier to answer. Still, the focus on representation in outputs was notably stark in the UK screen industries, whether in Diamond's analysis of on-screen diversity through 'perceived data' (CDN, 2021; see Section 5.2) or in the attention to diversity in narratives and stories (BFI, 2019; Channel 4, 2019a; see Section 2.4.) Moreover, across their D&I efforts, the screen industries also recognised a comparatively larger set of diversity characteristics as relevant. Diversity data was collected not only for the protected characteristics listed in the 2010 Equality Act but increasingly also for socio-economic background, caring responsibilities, geographical location or age.

These five headline findings from the initial research – D&I targets are part of the D&I picture in UK screen, but do not dominate it; D&I data reporting is more prominent than D&I target setting; the availability of D&I data is skewed towards workforce and on-screen diversity data; there is little systematic reflection on D&I targets; D&I targets in the UK screen industries are more nuanced than in other sectors – form the bigger picture for which the following sections provide more detail.

4.3 Diversity targets in the UK screen industries

The vast majority of D&I targets in the UK screen industries are diversity targets: workforce diversity targets, on-screen diversity targets or participant diversity targets. To briefly recap, diversity targets look at representation and variation. They ask how represented different variations of an individual characteristic (age, disability, sex/gender, race/ethnicity etc.) are within a group, that is, a workforce, the fictional and non-fictional individuals shown on-screen or the participants of an intervention or training, and compare the status quo to an aspirational future state of representation (Section 2.4).

Workforce diversity targets dominated the D&I publications we analysed. But not only were workforce targets by far the most the most common type of D&I targets, our research also found clear patterns of targets setting practice:

- Workforce diversity targets were most often set for gender and race/ethnicity. Targets for disability and sexual orientation were also common.
- Targets for class or socio-economic background were slowly emerging. Typical proxies used for measuring class or socio-economic background included parental occupation and type of school attended.
- Age targets were much less frequent, even though both baseline data and reference data would be readily available.
- Our research did not find concrete diversity targets for pregnancy and maternity, marriage and civil partnership or gender reassignment. D&I publications mentioned various interventions to improve return to work and work-life balance but without stating numerical targets.
- Reflecting the specific industry set-up, workforce diversity targets are used not only at company level but also at industry level or for individual productions. Commissioning broadcasters, for example, set workforce diversity targets for productions and CDN's Doubling Disability initiative set a cross-broadcaster, industry-level target for the share of disabled workers in off-screen broadcasting roles (CAMEo, 2019).

Notably, in the UK screen industries, workforce diversity targets seem to have moved on from considering only overall workforce figures. While overall figures are important and remained cited, they were typically complemented with analysis by career levels defined either by seniority or by pay (e.g. top 20 roles/top 100 paid staff). Targets for senior leaders or the highest paid staff most commonly focus on gender and race/ethnicity, and, more recently, disability.

The second prominent type of diversity targets in the UK screen industries were on-screen diversity targets. For TV, on-screen diversity is reported through Diamond (e.g. CDN, 2021). Concrete target setting for on-screen diversity happens most prominently in broadcasters' commissioning guidelines and the BFI Diversity Standards in film. Commissioning broadcasters and the BFI as a funder state on-screen diversity targets as conditions; that is, projects will not be commissioned or awarded funding if they do not meet these targets. Notably, these targets are transorganisational D&I targets, set by one organisation for another (see Section 2.6), and thus face the challenge of the target setting organisation not necessarily having a full view of how ambitious and achievable a target is for the target receiving organisation. Our research found two approaches to presenting on-screen targets. The first approach is for the target setting organisation to set overall targets they seek to fulfil across all commissions. An example of this approach was Sky's suite of diversity targets of 50% women and 20% individuals from Black, Asian and minoritised ethnic groups in lead and supporting roles and 10% on-screen people that audiences will perceive as disabled (Sky, 2020, 2022). A second approach to on-screen diversity targets was to give production companies a choice of on-screen targets to meet with the project they propose. This second approach was first taken by the BFI Diversity Standards and also incorporated into commissioning guidelines, for instance at Channel 4 and ITV (Channel 4, 2021; ITV, 2018). Channel 4, for instance, stipulated that scripted programmes had to have either 50% women lead characters or at least one lead character from an minoritised ethnic group or portrayed as disabled or LGBT (Channel 4, 2021a). This second approach can be, but was not always, linked to statements of overall on-screen diversity targets – an example would be the BFI's statement of overall diversity targets to achieve 'among our employees and within the filmmakers we support' (BFI, n.d.), which framed the more detailed Diversity Standard targets set for funding applicants. On-screen diversity targets seemed to be developing from overall targets to also include specific targets for lead characters or 'prominently featuring' presenters and contributors.

Finally, participant diversity targets relate to the representation of individuals with different characteristics amongst the participants of a training programme or intervention (see Section 2.3). Participant diversity targets were explicitly set by ScreenSkills and the BFI. Both organisations set targets for gender, ethnicity, disability and sexual orientation, and ScreenSkills also sets targets for socio-economic background and location.[1] The UK broadcasters' publications suggested that they aimed for participant diversity on at least some of their interventions but did not seem to set explicit participant diversity targets. Similar to ScreenSkills, some broadcasters run interventions that are completely or partially ring-fenced for participants with a particular characteristic. For example, in 2017, Channel 4's legal and compliance department held 50% of the places on their annual placement scheme for disabled students and lawyers (Channel 4, 2017).

4.4 Reference data for diversity target setting in the UK screen industries

Reference data can, in principle, be any data that an organisation wishes to compare their D&I status quo with, to ascertain if a D&I target might be a useful measure (see Section 3.3). In reality, the idea of representation dominates the screen industries' D&I conversation and influences the choice of reference data, too. A representation approach to reference data would ask: 'How are individuals from certain groups represented elsewhere and how should they therefore be represented in our workforce?'

Concrete information about how reference data for D&I targets is chosen and which datasets in particular are used was ambiguous in the UK screen industries. For workforce diversity, the most commonly mentioned reference data point was the UK working-age population. However, both in the context of reporting workforce diversity and of setting workforce diversity targets, D&I publications often referred only vaguely to data about 'the workforce' or 'the population'. Even where the Labour Force Survey (LFS) or 2011 Census data were mentioned, detailed information about which data from these sources was being used was missing. Notable exceptions were CDN and Ofcom, but with the exception of CDN's Doubling Disability initiative (CAMEo, 2019), CDN and Ofcom do not set D&I targets for workforce diversity in the UK screen industries.[2]

Target setting for on-screen diversity mirrors the conversation for workforce diversity. On-screen diversity targets are set to drive actions towards screen outputs that better reflect the make-up of the audiences. In line with this argument, where reference data was cited, general population statistics rather than working-age population or labour force were referred to. Here too though, we found no information on the exact data sources.

Importantly, even where reference data sources were stated, our research did not find information on how reference data was used to set target levels. The diversity targets published often deviated from the reference data values. A particularly prominent example was disability. Although disabled people make up 20% of the working-age population (Powell, 2021), workforce diversity, on-screen diversity and participant diversity targets typically ranged from 8% to 12%. These deviations might result from considerations around, for instance, achievability or, especially for race and ethnicity targets, regional difference. Without explicit information, however, it remains unclear how reference data was used in D&I target setting in the UK screen industries.

4.5   Workforce diversity target levels in the UK screen industries

Once our research had identified that D&I targets in the UK screen industries were mainly diversity targets – and, in particular, workforce diversity targets – we analysed the data for patterns in target levels. The first finding to note was that, at the time of our research, diversity target levels in the UK screen industries were set as percentage figures rather than target ranges.

- Targets for gender were typically set at 50% for women or 50/50 women/ men.
- Race and ethnicity targets showed some evolution over time. Initial target levels from around the 12% mark have gradually been increased to targets of 15% of the workforce to come from Black, Asian and minoritised ethnic backgrounds, and then to 20% for BFI, BBC, Channel 4, ITN and Sky (BFI, 2019; BBC, 2019a; Channel 4, 2019a; ITN, 2018a; Sky, 2021b). The

BFI has, from 2022, set the highest-level target for race and ethnicity at 40% for London and 30% outside London.

- Workforce diversity targets for disability show a similar evolution, from 6% to 8% to more recent targets set at 12%. The highest target for disability workforce representation for the reviewed period was 18%, set by Ofcom (Ofcom, 2017a) for its own workforce to reflect the proportion of disabled people in the working-age population in 2020.
- At the time of our research, disability was the only characteristic for which a cross-industry target existed. As part of CDN's Doubling Disability initiative, the Diamond broadcasters had committed to doubling the proportion of disabled people in off-screen roles by the end of 2021 to 9% (CAMEo, 2019).
- Targets related to sexual orientation or the proportion of LGBTQ+ people in the workforce ranged from 6% to 8% (with one older case of this target set at 2%), reflecting the proportion of LGBTQ+ people in the working-age population. For the period researched, 2010–2023, LGBTQ+ workforce diversity targets were the most likely to have already been met.
- Several publications mentioned religion and belief but only Ofcom specifically provided numerical targets or broad aims in relation to this characteristic, noting that there was a 67:26 spilt in the 2011 Census between people who declare a religion or belief and those who describe themselves as not having a religion or belief.
- Until very recently, concrete target setting for socio-economic diversity of the workforce was less frequent. Ofcom used to provide the most detailed data on social class, with an aim to have no more than one-third of their workforce with parents from professional occupations (based on parental occupation at the age of 14) and no more than 7% of the workforce having attended a private school (Ofcom, 2017a). The BBC initially monitored socio-economic background but noted low levels of declaration and the difficulties this lack of data presents for setting targets (BBC, 2018c). In their latest reports, the BBC and ITN have both set targets for 25% of their workforce to come from working-class backgrounds.

Across D&I publications, there was some discussion of adjustments to regional demographics or other location-specific aspects. Sky, for instance, advocated regional target setting and the BBC noted that international, regional and local teams might adjust targets in line with local audience demographics (Sky, 2021b). Ofcom provided a separate race/ethnicity benchmark for London-based functions (33% of the Ofcom workforce in London should be from a Black, Asian or minoritised ethnic group) (Ofcom, 2021), and ITN also noted a need to be aware of the geographic differences in relation to race and ethnicity. Channel 4 stated their aspiration to increase out-of-London content spending and briefings, and there was generally a recognition of the tension between the London-centric operating model of the screen industries and any aspirations for diversity, inclusion and representation (Channel 4, 2018).

4.6   Inclusion targets in the UK screen industries

Diversity targets and the rationales of representation clearly dominated the D&I target landscape in publications we analysed. Similarly, a 2021 study by the Creative Industries Policy & Evidence Centre (Carey et al., 2020) found that the majority of D&I interventions in the screen industry were targeted at the career entry stage of screen workers. In other words, the D&I ecology's actions focused on getting a more diverse group of workers into the screen industries.

That focus notwithstanding, the publications we analysed did also describe a broad range of D&I interventions intended to improve inclusion. Typical examples were recruitment trainings and unconscious bias trainings to improve decision-making in recruitment and promotion, for example, ITV's Inclusive Leader and Inclusive Hiring programmes (ITV, 2022a); data gathering initiatives such as Channel 4's campaign to increase disclosure (Channel 4, 2022b); awareness campaigns such as the BBC's in-depth reports on the experiences of women, disabled workers and workers from working-class and minoritised backgrounds (BBC, 2018c, 2018d, 2019b); or Channel 4's This Is Me campaign (Channel 4, 2019b). More recently, interventions such as the BFI's principles and guidance on anti-bullying and harassment (BFI, 2020a, 2020b) and the Film + TV Charity's Whole Picture Toolkit for mental health and wellbeing (Film and TV Charity, n.d.) sought to provide concrete advice on how to change industry practice and improve screen workers' experiences of and in work. The most common inclusion-focused intervention are staff networks in which people from under-represented groups can exchange their experiences, support each other and form a collective voice for advocating within their organisation. The most screen-specific example of inclusion-focused intervention were funding and commissioning guidelines that require production companies to consider on-screen portrayal and to actively work against stereotypical representation especially of under-represented ethnic groups. For example, Standard A of the BFI's Diversity Standards sets out criteria relating to 'non-stereotypical representations of characters, talent or contributors who are normally relegated to two-dimensional roles' and casting choices that 'challenge tropes and stereotypes' (BFI, 2019: 3).

Across this breadth of activity, it is less easy to systematically distinguish between clear inclusion targets and broader aims. To recap, inclusion targets, as defined in Section 2.4, relate to broader indicators of inclusive practice such as individual experiences, organisational interventions or on-screen narratives – that is, exactly to the kinds of outcomes the interventions described earlier seek to affect. Descriptions of such interventions would frequently be prefaced with statements such as 'We expect all content makers to come to us with ideas that already have diversity, representation and inclusion built into their development. Those that support our editorial strategy and our goals stand the greatest chance of being commissioned' (BBC, 2018h: 7). Such statements, however, are statements of intent rather than inclusion targets with explicitly stated and timebound outcomes. While descriptors of inclusion interventions may state the strategic or operational action through which outcomes are imagined to be affected, the statements of intent that proceed them lack the concrete detail required in a D&I target.

Our research did, however, find an emerging practice of setting inclusion targets that are more specific and timebound.

- *Pay gap targets*: Pay gap data were presented by various organisations using two measures: the absolute pay gap and the bonus pay gap. Pay gaps were usually presented by sex/gender and race/ethnicity. The general aim seemed to be progression towards completely closing the sex/gender or race/ethnicity pay gap. Mostly, this general aim was not explicitly stated; rather there seemed to be an underlying assumption that pay gaps on the basis of individuals' diversity should not exist. However, some organisations set themselves concrete, timebound pay gap-related targets, such ITN's 2018 intention to reduce the race/ethnicity pay gap by 50% by 2022 (ITN, 2018a, 2023).
- *On-screen portrayal targets*: As noted earlier, TV commissioning guides in particular requested that programmes should 'reflect' contemporary UK society or that programmes 'prominently feature' presenters or contributors from under-represented groups. In some cases, these statements of intent were phrased in a more concrete, target-type language, for example, Channel 4's activities around 'Developing Commissioning Genre Diverse Audience Strategies, in order to evolve how we authentically portray diverse groups on screen' (Channel 4, 2019a: 4). Similarly, the BBC made authentic portrayal one of the criteria for productions to count towards the BBC's Diversity Commitment (BBC, 2022a).
- *Intervention targets*: Intervention targets formalise an organisation's intention to undertake certain D&I interventions. The BBC, for instance, has committed to building an LGBTQ+ inclusive culture in which 50% of staff who identify as LGBTQ+ are comfortable to be 'open about their LGBTQ+ identity in the workplace' (BBC, 2021b: 17).
- *Investment targets*: Investment targets state budgets to be spent, for example, on D&I interventions, generally, on specific D&I programmes or on commissioning programmes with a particular D&I aspect. Because they used numerical formats and were linked to budget years, investment targets stood out as D&I targets that were related to diversity and inclusion, but were not, in themselves, diversity targets. For example, in 2021, Sky pledged to spend £10 million per year for the next three years to help tackle racial injustice (Sky, 2021a). More recently, Channel 4 (2022) introduced an investment target at production level, offering productions the choice of fulfilling a workforce diversity target for race/ethnicity and disability or demonstrating the salary spend for staff from these groups in off-screen roles exceeded a certain threshold.

These targets were likely more visible as inclusion targets to the researcher's gaze, using a particular lens and comparing target setting practice across the screen industries D&I ecology. From this perspective, patterns in the emerging industry practice are becoming clearly visible. At the time of writing, industry and policy makers would probably not systematically use the term inclusion targets to distinguish targets of the above four types from the diversity targets described in the previous Section 4.5. With explicit inclusion targets only cautiously emerging in D&I publications and strategies, lived industry experience will likely remain dominated by diversity targets and the issues surrounding those for the moment (see Section 2.3).

4.7   Challenges of D&I target setting

Throughout this book, I have highlighted where evidence and guidance are missing, and Chapter 5 will summarise the most pressing gaps. Of course some of the shortcomings of current practice and challenges of working with D&I targets are already being discussed across academic literature and industry conversation. This section will briefly review these issues.

A first set of challenges concerns the methods and practicalities of working with D&I targets. Publications noted that data sets were incomplete or that existing data collection systems did not provide the coverage that was ideally needed. They also noted that appropriate benchmark and reference data was not available and that there was not enough evaluation of 'what works' for delivering on D&I targets.

A second set of challenges relates to, broadly, the industry's understanding of diversity and inclusion and what it might take to improve both. Tokenism – doing something to be seen to be doing something – and a reliance on quick fixes were mentioned as getting in the way of substantive change. Another key concern raised in this context was that commitment from senior leaders was not always strong enough to sustain, let alone drive, the change of organisational cultures, systems and structures that D&I work requires. Connected to this idea of commitment was the notion of D&I work, including D&I targets, as a 'cost burden' – as something that did or might require more resource than especially small organisations could be expected to commit.

Some of these points, for instance the lack of commitment, were not what the *ScreenSkills D&I Targets Review* was designed to look at. Other points though, like the challenges of working with reference data, were also picked up by the *Review*'s analysis. Chapter 5 will therefore start with an exploration of next steps to address what the UK screen industries themselves recognise as challenges of 'doing D&I targets well'.

Notes

1 NB although the BFI sets transorganisational location/geography targets for other organisations, location targets are not listed in the BFI's D&I target overview online (BFI, n.d.).

2 Ofcom sets targets for its own workforce but as a UK government agency, its workforce would count towards the public sector rather than the screen industries.

5 What's next for D&I targets?

This final chapter starts by pointing out four knowledge gaps that currently hold back our use of D&I targets and outlines how we might plug those gaps. It then discusses the benefits and drawbacks of 'counting' people's characteristics in the name of D&I target setting. The chapter closes the book by arguing the case for inclusion targets, and by explaining how taking the perspective of inclusion seriously can improve the worlds we build together.

5.1 Work in progress

Throughout this book I have emphasised that our use of D&I targets is work in progress. It is 'work in progress' because of the current state of our understanding of D&I targets – of what they are, what they can be used for, and how we use them well. As the research that underpins this book has shown, we are by no means there yet in our ability to use D&I targets competently and responsibly, alert to their methodological and ideological workings and in service of those whose experiences we purportedly want to improve. The first section of this concluding chapter takes stock of what we know is missing, the known unknowns. It reviews the gaps in our D&I target literacy and the questions that will need answering next.

But when we work with D&I targets, we also work to progress. In this sense, the work in progress is the work of progressing to a more progressive place. A place in which D&I targets are much less, if at all, needed to ensure that people's opportunities and experiences as well as our collective connections are underpinned by the principles of equity, equality and inclusion. A place in which we appreciate and embrace difference rather than merely monitor it. The second and third section of this chapter ask more fundamental questions about working with D&I targets, about counting diversity and about imagining the places we might want to get to.

In the introduction, I have described the current situation as a lopsided one in which we pursue surface measures (diversity and diversity targets) rather than pay attention to the causes and dynamics (inclusion, or the lack of it) of

DOI: 10.4324/9781003434542-5

the things we want to tend to (people's opportunities and experiences, and our collective connections). The following three sections go beyond, in some moments significantly beyond, the research undertaken as part of the *Review* for ScreenSkills. My aim here is to position the work that this book seeks to do in rebalancing our current lopsidedness and in getting our thinking and doing onto a path towards, one day, finally, living and working without D&I targets.

5.2   Known unknowns

The evidence we have on how D&I targets are being and should be used is limited and uneven. The research undertaken for the *ScreenSkills D&I Targets Review* and updated for this book found little relevant academic literature. Our search of publication databases with the basic, not screen-specific combination of search words '(diversity OR inclusion) AND (target)' in the title or abstract of academic research papers returned a healthy 1208 results but only eight of those were relevant to the specific topic of D&I targets covered in this book.[1] The industry reports reviewed stated D&I-related aims or objectives (e.g. of improving on-screen representation of disabled people) but gave notably less detail on explicit, timebound targets. Most attention in both academic research and industry reports is focused on workforce diversity targets.

With so much evidence missing, it would be tempting to call for more research on D&I targets full stop. But the idea of, let's call it 'a large-scale, academia-industry evidence improvement campaign', is not a solely benign one – I will discuss why in more detail later. Instead of mapping all we could know but currently do not, I will therefore outline four points at which our current knowledge genuinely limits how good (as in how meaningful, competent and effective at driving change) our work with D&I targets can be.

First, formats. We observe notably more activity and evidence where there are comparatively established formats for expressing and monitoring D&I targets. Consider on-screen diversity and pay gap targets. On-screen diversity targets work with perceived data (i.e. how viewers might interpret a character on screen) instead of diversity data declared by individuals about themselves. But in their underlying logic, on-screen diversity targets are a comparatively straightforward extension of workforce diversity targets: same principle (How many of which?) applied to a different population (on-screen as opposed to in the workforce) regarding aspects of screen industry activity that are undoubtedly relevant to diversity and inclusion (Who is visible on screen? Who gets to work on screen?). Pay gap reporting is, in the United Kingdom, currently only mandatory for gender, and only for companies with more than 250 employees. Nevertheless, in the UK screen industries its established formats (difference between women's and men's mean and median hourly pay and bonuses) have quickly been applied to pay gap reporting for race, disability or full-time versus part-time contracts, including with explicit pay gap targets (e.g. ITN, 2023). Unlike for other inclusion targets, access to data is comparatively easy and there are clear reporting formats for pay gaps – including format choices (e.g. mean vs. median, including/excluding freelancers) for supporting a particular argument. Both of these examples suggest that where there are established formats in circulation and data access is (perceived to be) easy, we will likely see greater use of D&I targets. Consequently, developing and establishing formats for inclusion targets should help increase their use and reporting.

Second, evidence of target setting processes. To better understand how D&I targets work and work well, and to make recommendations for their use, we need better insight into the mechanics of setting D&I targets. We need more information about the data that is being used – both baseline and reference data – and about the processes and decision-making rationales that transform data into targets. Which data we work with determines whether, frankly, targets make sense. At the moment, evidence of how data is chosen and guidance for how data should be chosen is thin. It may have sufficed for getting us to the current status quo, but current level evidence and guidance on data use are unlikely to support next steps.

Insight and evidence are also thin where D&I target setting touches the bigger picture of D&I strategy. At that interface live questions about rationales and decision-making, for instance, which diversity characteristics to set targets for, how big a gap between baseline and reference data needs to be to trigger target setting, or when a target might be dropped because it counts as fulfilled. The answers to these questions should come from overarching D&I policies or strategies that D&I targets should act in service of. However, we currently have little evidence of how those connections are made. If anything in the UK screen industries we can observe a disconnect between the leitmotiv of addressing under-representation (see Section 5.3) and the absence of workforce diversity targets for age or caring responsibilities, for which the gap between overall workforce representation figures and reference data points is arguably bigger than for, say, gender or sexual orientation.[2] D&I targets have opportunity costs. Because they require action to achieve, they attract attention, effort and – more often than not – budgets, and in doing so de-tract those finite resources from other D&I causes. In this way, D&I targets create a focus in our D&I work – a focus that should be conscious and aligned with an overarching strategy rather than an implicit, accidental side effect. For instance, if the strategic aim is to improve inclusion, setting only diversity targets creates an incongruousness between the overall aim and the focusing of finite resources that diversity targets will effect. What is needed here are frameworks that translate strategic D&I aims and that operationalise abstract, complex rationales like 'equitable allocation of opportunity and outcome' or 'inclusive decision-making' for meaningful D&I target setting.

Third, transorganisational target setting. D&I targets currently used in the UK screen industries comprise both internal D&I targets (targets set by an organisation for itself, e.g. for improving diversity amongst its workforce) and transorganisational D&I targets (targets set by one organisation for one or more other organisations, e.g. through commissioning or funding). However, academic research and industry conversations about the specific dynamics of transorganisational D&I target setting and how these dynamics might be taken into account do not feature prominently. These knowledge gaps are relevant not only for the screen industries. Making access to something conditional on activities related to D&I is an important policy lever. Arts Council England and Creative Scotland, for instance, require the submission of diversity data as a condition of funding. Outside the creative industries, the National Institute for Health Research has for years required funding applicants to hold a Silver Award of the Athena Swan Charter (e.g. Advance HE, 2020).[3] While organisation theory and neo-institutional economics have obvious analytical frameworks on offer, what is likely more needed is industry-led, systematic reflection on designing insightful conversations about what achievability and ambition in target setting and target delivery mean for both the target setting organisation and the organisation receiving the target. Our research suggests that clarity of definitions (e.g. what are diversity targets, what are inclusion targets and what functions do they fulfil?) and transparency about processes (e.g. how is reference data used to set target levels?) will be essential for those conversations.

Fourth, unintended consequences. The next two sections will explore in more detail the side effects of working with diversity data and focusing on under-representation. It is worth drawing attention here to the lack of conversation about unintended consequences of D&I target setting more broadly though. Currently the only established discussion in this regard concerns voluntary targets versus mandatory quotas (e.g. for boardroom-level interventions: CIPD, 2015; Kang et al., 2023; Mensi-Klarbach et al., 2021; Oldford, 2021; for race and ethnicity: McGregor-Smith Review, 2017; more generally Noon and Ogbonna, 2021). Academic research and industry/policy publications point out that mandatory quotas have the potential to cause resentment, including among employers who are responsible for implementing them, and can stigmatise individuals who are appointed to meet them (CIPD, 2015). An illustrative example is the German term 'Quotenfrau' ('quota woman', i.e. a woman allocated a position to meet a quota for women) which still carries such deeply entrenched negative connotations that a good 40 years after quotas for women started to become more widely used, the leading magazine *stern* ran a campaign in which 40 woman leaders 'outed' themselves as a Quotenfrau to demonstrate the benefits that quotas can bring (Stawski et al., 2020).

There are also emerging reflections on the use of workforce diversity targets, pointing out that 'focus[ing] only on increasing minority representation in [the] workplace, there is a danger of neglecting the underlying climate of support and inclusion' (CIPD, 2018: 22) or that 'diversity fatigue' (Channel 4, 2019a: 22) can set in if progress as assessed by representation measures is perceived to be slow. But more systematic accounts of how working with D&I targets shapes individual and organisational practice, especially in unexpected or counterproductive ways, are missing. Which, given that targets are set to shape actions, means that we are lacking important insight into how targets can and do work, and how we can and do work with targets. We are not quite operating with a black box model of D&I targets; we can see targets being stated. But much of the everyday reality of setting targets and working to achieve them – or attempting to game them – is still not well evidenced, certainly not in the screen industries (see Noon and Ogbonna's (2021) case study outwith screen for an example of the type of insights needed). It would be much preferable to replace current assumptions about how people might engage and react with robust insight into the actions and behaviour change that occur in and as a consequence of D&I target setting.

For all four of these points, academic research can undoubtedly support the gathering of good-quality evidence and bring in frameworks – for instance on incentive setting, decision-making and behaviour change in organisational contexts – that have proved insightful elsewhere. Chiefly though, these points will need to be addressed through cross-industry conversation, through a joint effort of sector organisations and employers as well as unions and campaigners, and prioritising insight into the everyday practices and decision-making in industry that provide the 'live habitat' in which D&I targets are envisaged to do their work.

Finally but importantly, a health warning. The above points ask for more evidence and better knowledge, and thus for time, attention and budget spent reflecting and improving methods, processes and practices. Many industry publications echo this call (e.g. CAMEo, 2018). We do need those improvements for D&I targets to be effective tools and, as Section 5.3 will explain in more detail, to reduce the possibility of causing harm to individuals and groups, especially those who have already endured the exclusion and discrimination that result from sexism and misogyny, disablism, racism, homophobia or transphobia, to name but some common culprits. There is, however, a danger that our attempts to plug knowledge gaps generate better data and improve our methods and processes stall progress rather than facilitate it. The danger is that instead of pursuing better data, methods and knowledge while *in parallel* working with our current tools as effectively and responsibly as we can until better ones arrive, we postpone any intervention or change until we have found 'perfect' methodological or procedural solutions. There is even an incentive for industry and policy to invest in plugging data and knowledge gaps in lieu of change interventions: the latter are notoriously more difficult to pull off, politically and practically, than the former, and thus a potentially much more palatable option for 'demonstrating commitment' to diversity and inclusion. We cannot let the mission for perfect get in the way of achieving the improvements we can already achieve on the basis of 'good enough' methods and evidence.

If we take a single-track approach focused on plugging knowledge gaps and developing evidence and methods, we run the risk of colluding in what Ruha Benjamin terms the 'datafication of injustice' (2022: 35). The 'hunt for more and more data about things we already know much about' (Benjamin, ibid.) keeps us from acting on our knowledge and actually improving equality. More and more comprehensive evidence of, in Benjamin's example, the deadly consequences of racism and racial inequalities does not reduce or prevent harm. Similarly, my recommendations for using evidence to improve diversity in the UK screen industries cautioned an industry and policy summit that 'we need[ed] to pick our battles and choose when to fight over statistics and evidence, and when to fight with them' (Eikhof, 2019). These same logics apply to working with D&I targets and their underlying data collection methods. Our current state of understanding and insight is insufficient, undoubtedly so, and needs to be improved. At the same time, the evidence we can gather is always infinite and our methods and processes are always improvable. There is a danger in focusing all our attention and budget on finding the 'correct' reference data or perfect target setting process. Some methodological improvements can be implemented straight away, and where that is possible, we need to do so. Where improvements will take a while to develop, we will have to, in parallel, use our existing methods as responsibly as we can to set sensible targets and act on them, so that we, in Benjamin's words, 'do what we can in the here and now to eliminate the sources of harm' (2022: 34).

5.3 Diversity targets and the dark side of visibility

Most of the D&I targets set are diversity targets, and especially workforce diversity targets. So far this book has mainly considered questions of focus (workforce, on-screen representation, training participation) or process (baseline data, reference data, target levels etc.). But to really understand how diversity targets work, we also need to look into the methods that underpin them. Diversity targets deal in representation: they are based on counting variation of a particular characteristic in a group. To set and work towards diversity targets, we need to, in statistical terms, establish the distribution of values for a particular variable in a population (see Sections 2.2 and 3.4) and then figure out what those values should ideally be. With that underlying counting we transform a social practice (e.g. the different ways in which people relate to religion, belief and spirituality and how that positions them in our collective relations) into quantitative statistics (e.g. A% atheist, B% Buddhist, C% Christian etc.). These acts of counting and 'tallying up' statistical measures are not inconsequential. When we count, we do not merely put into practice numeracy skills acquired through nursery rhymes and primary school math lessons. Counting in itself 'does something' to how we understand diversity and diversity targets – and how we act on, and with, both of them. This section will start to connect our conversation on diversity data and targets with the rich literature that explores how data and counting shape lives (see D'Ignazio and Klein (2020) for a comprehensive introduction into the many aspects I do not have space to discuss in detail here). I will continue to use 'we' but with an extension of my introductory remarks (see Chapter 1) about who that 'we' is imagined to be. In Chapter 1, I noted that with 'we' I refer to a diverse group of people who take different and at times opposing positions within conversations about diversity and inclusion, let alone equity, social justice, human rights and abolition. As will become clearer in the below, that part of the 'we' that is doing the counting and that part of the 'we' which is being counted are not just differentiated by differences in perception but also by differences in the power they hold and (can) use to shape their own and others' experiences. These differences matter greatly and materially to people's lives. The reason I persist with 'we' despite those real-live differences is a doggedly hopeful, conceptual one: I do not want to lose sight of the fact that it is still one 'we' and that we are hurting ourselves when one part of that 'we' does something to another part of that 'we' that is harmful, discriminating, exclusionary.

At the most basic level, when we count the representation of individuals with a specific characteristic in a group, we create a way of describing – in absolute or relative figures – 'what diversity looks like' in a group. In that description, individual experiences of being denied access become visible as a collective status quo of under-representation. Diversity and under-representation are problems of scale, and, usefully, quantitative statistics are powerful methods for describing such problems of scale (D'Ignazio and Klein, 2020). It is precisely this capacity of quantitative data that makes diversity statistics of value to policy makers and campaigners. 'The worlds of policy and policy making run on data', as Kevin Guyan (2022: 168) points out. Only what is visible can be addressed, actioned and acted upon (e.g. Bacchi and Goodwin, 2016; Eikhof et al., 2019). Diversity data statistics make under-representation and discrimination recognisable as more than individual anecdotes, and in doing so, they make these problems actionable. Once a problem is visible and actionable it can be addressed by industry and policy.

Visibility and recognisability are created through the methods and definitions used for counting, through the analysis applied to the data and through the formats used for presenting the information (e.g. D'Ignazio and Klein, 2020; Law et al., 2011). When we design the surveys with which we collect individual information, our decisions about which questions to include create visibility for diversity characteristics and for people's identities. Which is why the first-time inclusion of sexual orientation and transgender identity questions in the 2022 Scottish Census was welcomed by queer rights groups and government agencies alike as making Scotland's queer community visible (Guyan, 2021a). But visibility always also creates invisibility; when we count for inclusion we exclude at the same time. To give the two most obvious examples: we create invisibility when we decide what to count and how we construct the categories we use in counting. Counting some individual characteristics (e.g. sex/gender, race, disability) and not others (caring responsibilities, refugee status, language, experience of the care system or domestic violence) makes the former visible markers of diversity and renders the latter invisible, and the inequalities relating to them unactionable. Depending on how we define knowledge work, for instance, certain gender gaps become visible in workforce statistics – and therefore actionable – and others do not (Walby, 2011). Similarly, if we follow the more mainstream path of using a collective label for sexual orientation, LGB diversity in the UK broadcasting workforce is more than twice as high as in the UK population (16% and 6.4%, respectively; CDN, 2023). A closer look, however, shows the 16% to be composed of 9% gay men and much smaller shares of individuals who identify as lesbian, bisexual or other. This much more complex picture of LGB representation is invisible from the overall figure – and therefore unactionable.

How we count also affords specific ways of being seen, of expressing and experiencing one's identity and denies others. Diversity initiatives open doors and provide entry, but that entry is only granted on the condition that one accepts how identity characteristics have been defined and are being operated (Ahmed, 2023). Crucially, the options for declaring our identity characteristics may or may not represent our own experience of our identity. The answer options for questions presented in the 2022 Scottish Census meant that those identifying as other than woman or man only became visible and recognisable on the terms that the gender-mainstream majority wanted to recognise them with – which did not necessarily correspond with their lived gender identity, which is what the census set out to record (Guyan, 2021b). This point is not a merely conceptual one: if our aim is not just to count, but to improve people's experiences of being included in a space, whether we do or do not offer them visibility, recognition and inclusion as the person they understand themselves to be, whether regarding their gender identity, race, religion, disability or other aspects of their identity, matters greatly.

And yet, visibility and recognisability (on whosever terms) is not always wholly benign, enabling or empowering either. Instead, as Catherine D'Ignazio and Lauren Klein (2020) point out, 'being visible . . . poses significant risks to the health and safety of minoritised groups'. In the United States, for instance, being openly recognised as transgender restricts how individuals can access health care, housing and finance (Lowder et al., 2023; D'Ignazio and Klein, 2020). A further chilling example comes from an exhibit I spotted in 2005 at the Belvedere in Vienna: a list of citizens to be arrested and deported because of their religious or political characteristics which was handed over to the Nazi administration within hours of the Anschluss. To be available so swiftly, the list must have been based on prior records that made individuals visible as belonging to certain groups – with, in this case, fatal consequences. These examples may appear far-fetched to those of us who have never experienced the material, physical or psychological consequences of discrimination. But they reveal a vulnerability that results from being visible and recognisable to exclusionary, discriminatory and harmful systems that will, sadly, resonate only too well with those of us who have had their career and life prospects curtailed by the racist, disablist, sexist, ageist, homophobic, transphobic, classist etc. perceptions and actions of others.

Setting D&I targets, and in particular diversity targets, takes these fundamental considerations about counting and diversity data to another level. Targets, as I have emphasised throughout this book, are set to instigate action. Counting creates visibility and recognisability and thus potential actionability. Target setting, by its very nature, starts where that potentiality leaves off: it initiates and drives action; it seeks to make action mandatory. And in doing so, target setting entrenches the visibilities, invisibilities and understandings of diversity that the methods of counting it builds upon have created. That is why we need to understand how counting works and what it does to our understanding of diversity and inclusion, and to our pursuit of improving both.

As one example, consider how we define diversity characteristics when setting D&I targets. If we use the currently most common category for counting racial identity, 'Black, Asian and minority ethnic', racial diversity in the UK broadcasting workforce looks on par with racial diversity in the UK population (13.9% and 13%, respectively; CDN, 2023). But within those 13.9%, high share of individuals identifying as 'mixed race' and, to a lesser extent, 'Black' drives representation. People who identify as Asian and who make up 7% of the UK population account for less than half of that in the broadcasting workforce (ibid.). If a workforce diversity target for 'Black, Asian and minority ethnic' were set at the level of the population figure, this target would be judged to be achieved while under-representation and experiences of exclusion for parts of the thus counted groups would continue. In this example, some of the inequalities that diversity targets for race were brought in to address would likely persist not despite the target but, at least partly, *because* of it – because of the way race and ethnicity are would, in this example, be counted and made (in)visible and thus (un)actionable in D&I target setting.

Discussing the visibility that counting and target setting creates (or withholds) through the lens of potential limitations and harms should make us do at least two things. First, it should make us reflect on data collection. Who can and should we ask to disclose information about their individual characteristics? What do they stand to gain or lose by doing so? What do we ask them to disclose and how? Are the processes and rules that govern how we collect, analyse and report data adequate? Is there a trade-off between the risks an individual might face in disclosing their personal identity data and the potential gains for a group of people with a specific characteristic? Is it appropriate to expect that individuals are willing to participate in diversity data collection and to even predicate participation in our collective endeavours on that expectation of willingness to count and be counted? Kevin Guyan (2022) offers a more detailed set of questions (see also D'Ignazio and Klein, 2020).

Second, our more informed perspective on counting and visibility should make us examine the circumstances under which it is appropriate to inflict the visibility that a diversity target creates on a group of individuals in the first place. We understand the under-representation that counting reveals as a sign that 'something is not quite right', that people are not in a space that they should be in. Setting diversity targets sets an incentive to get the currently missing people into the space or, as it is more commonly expressed, 'to improve representation'. What counting alone does not do is draw attention to the space itself, and, crucially, to the reasons why certain people are not in it. Without that second step, setting diversity targets is essentially an exercise of inviting people into a space that we know – or would know, if we paused to think about it – is not (yet) right for them. We are starting to see conversations about the unintended consequences of D&I interventions, including targets. But what those conversation do not prominently say is that *the very first step*, the *initial practice of setting diversity targets* to improve representation creates an incentive to invite into a space those who have a higher-than-average likelihood of being harmed in that space by persisting homophobia or transphobia, for instance, or by heteronormative, patriarchal, classist perspectives. Setting a diversity target makes people visible as potential recipients of an invitation to step into situations that we know are disproportionately more likely to harm them. Have we considered the moral implications of creating that visibility? Have we considered who creates it and wherefrom they draw the moral justification to set targets and create visibility? Do we know if those we invite in as part of our quest to improve our diversity count will feel obliged to accept our invitation, if they will be able to make an informed choice about the likely risks that doing so carries?

When we set diversity targets we do not, as I hope this section has shown, merely deal in numbers. We deal in people whose identities and lives become subject to socially constructed and politically contested ways of counting, representing and shaping the groups that make up our organisations, businesses, interventions and projects. Our approach to target setting needs to do justice to these complexities and the power relationships and contested meanings that underpin them.

5.4   Inclusion: To boldly go . . . where, exactly?

The driving rationale behind the setting of diversity targets has been to address under-representation. Over 15 years of analysing policy and evidence for the UK creative industries, I have seen the problem of under-representation, the idea that people from certain groups or with certain individual characteristics are not included in our workforces or on our screens as they should be, centred time and time again (e.g. CAMEo, 2018; Guyan and Eikhof, forthcoming). Throughout such D&I strategies and industry reports, the leitmotif of fighting under-representation is, implicitly more than explicitly, used to justify diversity targets (e.g. BBC, 2022b; Channel 4, 2022b; ITV, 2021; Ofcom, 2021d). In this section, I want to unpack the workings of that leitmotif and the focus on diversity targets: how they shape our approach to D&I targets now, and, importantly, how they influence our future approach to D&I targets.

The under-representation leitmotif starts with the highlighting of a – statistically measured – non-diverse status quo and the labelling of that status quo as in need of remedying. We point at percentages and say 'this is wrong, we do not want that, we have to change it'. This act of establishing under-representation as existing and in need of addressing is an important task in itself, and one that has taken us longer to accomplish than we might think. Until as late as 2016, gender inequality and the under-representation of women mainly featured in screen industry research and policy as 'something that needed evidencing rather than changing' (Eikhof et al., 2019: 851). Only recently, and likely catalysed by the #MeToo and #BlackLivesMatter movements, have questions of how to effectively address under-representation come more to the fore (Eikhof et al., forthcoming). Establishing under-representation as actionable and to be actioned takes time. Much of this time is spent focusing on the status quo – although, as Shelley Cobb (2020) points out, on the status quo of the under-represented while the over-represented majorities remain largely invisible.

In D&I target setting, this focus on the status quo of representation has, in my observation, been fortified by the status quo of our collective ability to use reference data for analysing representation. That ability has yet to advance beyond comparatively basic levels (Sections 3.3 and 4.4). Practicalities will play a role here: If, for sake of argument, the current representation of disabled people in off-screen broadcasting roles is multiples off both national population and labour force figures (6.5% (CDN, 2023) as opposed to 17.7% (ONS, 2023b) and 23% (House of Commons Library, 2023), respectively), we can point towards that gap and call for change without debating which reference data 'correctly' describes the representation we should see. Over the past decades, workforce diversity figures for the UK screen industries have deviated so considerably from any halfway sensible reference point that the political task of justifying and affecting action did simply not require more accurately identified representation targets – and our lack of reference data understanding has disincentivised asking for more accuracy. Addressing the status quo offered a much more appealing return-on-investment ratio for time and effort than diving into detailed reference data statistics.

However understandable, the focus on evidencing and highlighting under-representation at the core of our D&I target setting has also had an important consequence: it has made thinking and talking about what we do *not* want the default position of our D&I conversation. We have an explicit agreement that we do not want under-representation (however defined) based on an implicit agreement that under-representation likely results from discrimination on the basis of individual characteristics that should not matter in the workplace. And of course it is important to understand (under-)representation and the harmful impacts of discrimination. We do need to attend to both. But we also need to acknowledge that in focusing on diversity and under-representation, our current conversations are dominated by the theme of 'this is wrong, we do not want that, we have to change it'.

We are now, slowly, beginning to question how we should use reference data in diversity target setting. In other words, we are starting to ask 'what would good representation look like?' I welcome these questions. Our attempts at answering them can generate a healthy conversation about the rigorous use of reference data and diversity data more generally, and that conversation should raise our D&I game on a number of fronts. ScreenSkills therefore deserve a special mention for commissioning the *D&I Targets Review* and using it to push the academia-industry-policy dialogue on D&I targets. I am keenly aware though that asking 'what would good representation look like?' is not the same as asking: 'what would good look like overall, how will we get there and how will we know when we've got there?' And it is the latter question that I believe we must turn a bigger slice of our attention to.

To genuinely meaningfully and impactfully set D&I targets we need a proper conversation about where we would like to get to. For that, we need to start thinking about inclusion and what it means to us. Unlike diversity, inclusion forces us much more quickly to consider not just what we do *not* want, but what we *do* want – how we *do* want to come together, collaborate and connect, allocate opportunities and outcomes? The title of this section is not a reference to Star Trek, but to the US disability rights campaigners who paraphrased the Star Trek mission to point out that their campaign for the Americans with Disabilities Act was merely asking for disabled people 'to boldly go where everyone else has gone before' (e.g. Golightley and Holloway, 2017). For me, the campaigners' slogan points to the frustrations and despair that await if we let the leitmotiv of representation (or, more specifically in the case of disability inclusion, the idea of access) limit our imagination of where we really want and could to get to. The under-representation leitmotif has considerable viability and staying power. Precisely because as a concept, diversity is of limited reach and meaning, we can, to an extent, get away with a surface-level engagement. Making inclusion a central paradigm asks more of us, and it does so more immediately. If we find our processes or practices to be exclusionary, it will likely not be feasible to merely ask colleagues to stop them – to not run events, not recruit, not hold meetings. We will need to offer inclusive alternatives – how to run an event inclusively, recruit inclusively, meet inclusively. Inclusion, as a perspective on our practices, structures, relationships, provisions, allocations, communications etc., has a generative, world-making quality: it asks us to envisage better solutions, to negotiate them and to collectively bring them into being. Taken seriously and not just as a label that accompanies the D-word (diversity) on report covers and in conference titles, inclusion asks us to question and rebuilt our systems and societies instead of merely offering better representation in the existing ones. In doing that, inclusion does not ignore under-representation and diversity targets, but it reaches beyond them.[4]

To offer one example of how inclusion extends the perspective beyond diversity and under-representation, consider a less prominently discussed side effect of attending to discrimination as part of attending to under-representation. Entwined with the idea that discrimination on the basis of some characteristics is unlawful in the workplace is the assumption that discrimination on the basis of other characteristics is justified. That there is an objective set of characteristics on the basis of which we can and should discriminate when we allocate opportunity or outcome in work. Skills, talent or merit are typical examples of such characteristics. By and large we accept skills, talent or merit as criteria for allocating opportunity and outcome because we believe that they are relevant to our workplaces, that they are objectively defined and that they can be developed and diagnosed in an individual to the point that they become the properties of the individual. A rich literature that I can merely point towards here unveils these beliefs as also problematic (for overviews, see Banks, 2017, 2023). In a myriad of ways, skill, talent and merit are socially constructed and context dependent. They are not something that is merely 'down to the person' and an objective basis for allocating someone their 'fair dues and just desserts' (Banks, 2023: 48). The 'level of acclaim' attributed to a professional pianist, for instance, is highly dependent on having a handspan wide enough to comfortably cover an octave on a standard keyboard. Women's hands are much less likely to have that handspan and women therefore less likely to be 'diagnosed' as talented pianists (Boyle et al. (2015) cited in Criado Perez, 2019). Such examples raise questions about how we understand talent, skill and merit, and if the ways in which we operationalise them currently are what we would want them to be. If we remain in our default position of focusing our attention on the under-representation and discrimination that we do not want, these problems do not come into view. Instead, through re-emphasising the discrimination we do *not* want we, implicitly but powerfully, also reiterate that it *is* justified to discriminate on the basis of talent, skill and merit as they are commonly understood. It is only when we interrogate what we do want rather than what we do not want that the more ambiguous nature of skill, talent and merit comes into view and that we can reflect on how we want to consider skills, talent and merit in our decision. Only from this perspective can we start to question on the basis of which criteria, and through which processes, we want to differentiate and discriminate between individuals. In other words, only when we leave our default position of focusing on the status quo can we envision the inclusive processes of allocating opportunities and outcomes that we might want to bring into being – and the targets we can set to help bring that change about.

Envisioning inclusive destinations and defining targets for getting there takes us onto new ground. We need to define where we want to go and how we will know when we got there. In Law et al'.s (2011: 12) words, we need to 'excavate the versions of the social embedded in our methods': work out which worlds our current D&I policies and target setting practices seek to bring into being and discuss how desirable those worlds actually are, what they might be missing and what we need to add in and work towards. As our research has shown, we already use some targets that set us on course for more inclusion. Pay gap targets, for instance, take a perspective beyond 'who gets in?' (representation) and ask 'what do they get out of their participation, is that equitable, are differences justified?' Granted, our current practices of setting pay gap targets are founded on assumptions about merit that can also be questioned, and they are a long way off alternative principles such as contributive justice (Banks, 2023). And of course views will differ on how desirable such alternative principles are in the first place. Nevertheless, querying outcomes can help turn our gaze beyond current under-representation and towards what could and should be more broadly. Similarly, inclusion targets for D&I interventions draw attention to the processes and practices we do want our organisations to be structured by. They ask which alternatives we would prefer to current exclusionary practice. Surveying employee's confidence in complaints procedures or sense of belonging (e.g. Advertising Association, 2021) can be a step towards operationalising a more inclusive state of being and doing, and towards setting targets for achieving that state. There might, of course, still be a place in this inclusion-driven perspective for measuring representation and for setting diversity targets – as long as we first ask ourselves the question 'what will good representation (however defined) be the symptom of?' Used in this way, representation and diversity become means to a more desirable end rather than the end in themselves that we currently tend to treat them as.

Inclusion is a much less understood and actionable goal and, unlike diversity, requires working out *what* we want rather than what we do *not* want. These conversations should be exciting, world-building, imagining; 'widening the script' as Sara Ahmed puts it, and 'tell[ing] each other stories of different ways you can live, different lives you can be' (Ahmed, 2017: 265). These conversations are also proper work. They require multidisciplinary thinking and negotiations about how we, as individuals and communities, want to come together, interact with one another and connect to achieve collective goals. Such questions reach well beyond common management or human resource management textbooks into fundamental debates of value, morals, health and wellbeing, resources, fairness, affordability, justice and sustainability – they are questions that 'need to be as complicated as the inequalities they attempt to address' (Eddo-Lodge, 2018: 183). These questions also extend well beyond the remit of any EDI unit or HR department in any organisation. They require a 'cultivation of common ground or indeed the re-imagining of the commons' (Dabiri, 2021: 146) more than correctly executed Equality Impact Assessments (UK Parliament, 2020).

Inclusion targets, if we develop them in the way described in this book, can help us with these conversations under two conditions. First, that we take the world-building, generative mandate of inclusion as an idea seriously and engage a broad perspective of voices and imaginations to figure out what we do want, where we do want to get to. Second, that we do not pour our attention solely into conversations about 'correct' methods for working with diversity data and reference data and fall into the trap of Benjamin's datafication of injustice (see Section 3.2). We need to improve our methods and then use them, especially our measures of representation, responsibly, cognisant of their limitations. But it cannot be an either/or. We need attention and resource to also be on reworking our collective connections in genuinely inclusive ways and take seriously the dangers of endless methodological debates from the depth of which we can, at best, pull up improved surface measures. What is more important is figuring out where, collectively, we want to go, and to set ourselves targets for how to get there. I hope that this book will encourage us to at least aim to do so. Are we nearly there yet? Well, no, we are not. But in the much more beautifully written words of Emma Dabiri (2021: 150):

> There are no quick fixes, but don't lose hope; ... As many of us as possible must embark on the journey. There are many others already well travelled; come let us find them, our fellow fugitives, redouble their efforts, and together dance under new suns glorious and unknown.

Notes

1 To reiterate the point I made in Chapter 1: there is, of course, literature on D&I aims and goals generally, and in particular research that analysis correlations between gender quotas and soft gender targets on the gender composition of company boards (illustratively Denis, 2022; Jaishiv, 2022; Kang et al., 2023; Mensi-Klarbach et al., 2021; Oldford, 2022; Viviers et al., 2022). What we have not been able to find is an established discussion of the types of workforce, participant and on-screen (or equivalent) diversity targets or the more broadly defined inclusion targets as used in the UK screen industries: which terms they use and why, how they are set, how they are worked with, what the challenges, unintended consequences and remaining knowledge gaps are.

2 For example, the Ukie 2022 Census (Taylor, 2022) reports that (1) 4% of people working in the games industry are aged 51 or over compared with LFS figures (ONS, 2023c) which show that 32% of the overall workforce are 50 or over, and (2) 22% of the games workforce have childcare responsibilities which it compares to 38% of the workforce overall who have dependent children.

3 In 2020, the NIHR changed this funding requirement and applicants now have to demonstrate a broader commitment to equality, diversity and inclusion, that is, beyond gender (e.g. Advance HE, 2020).

4 I want to emphasise that my use of 'inclusion' or 'inclusive practice' does not mean opening up participation in existing discriminatory, harmful or exploitative systems to more of us. Such a shallow notion of inclusion is rightly being criticised widely, including by writers cited in this chapter (e.g. Ahmed, 2023; Benjamin, 2022; Dabiri, 2021; Eddo-Lodge, 2018). Much of our current realities are in need of revising and rebuilding, so that the practices, structures, relationships, provisions, allocations, communications etc. that make our societies are experienced as open, participative, connecting, empathic, respectful of difference and equitably designed, by everyone. Rather than abandoning the term inclusion for its often shallow, myopic use to affirm existing systems I prefer, for now at least, to keep using the I-word and claim it for a more powerful form of social change.

References

The following lists all sources cited in the text and, marked with (*), all industry reports analysed for the *ScreenSkills D&I Targets Review*.

Abdul, G. (2023) 'The return of #BaftasSoWhite, three years after diversity outcry', *The Guardian*, 20 Feb. www.theguardian.com/film/2023/feb/20/the-return-of-baftassowhite-three-years-after-diversity-outcry [Accessed 3 Jul 2023].

Advance HE (2020) 'Advance HE responds to the NIHR's announcement on funding criteria', *Athena Swan | Advance HE*. advance-he.ac.uk [Accessed 27 Jul 2023].

Advertising Association (2021) 'All in report & action plan'. https://advertisingallin.co.uk/wp-content/uploads/2023/05/FINAL-ALL-IN-ACTION-PLAN-UPDATED-9-ACTIONS.pdf [Accessed 19 Aug 2023].

Ahmed, S. (2007) 'The language of diversity', *Ethnic and Racial Studies*, 30(2), pp. 235–256. DOI: 10.1080/01419870601143927

Ahmed, S. (2017) *Living a Feminist Life*, Durham and London: Duke University Press.

Ahmed, S. (2023) *The Feminist Killjoy Handbook*, London: Allen Lane.

Alvarez, J. L., Mazza, C., Pedersen, J. S., and Svejenova, S. (2005) 'Shielding idiosyncrasy from isomorphic pressures: Towards optimal distinctiveness in European filmmaking', *Organization*, 12(6), pp. 863–888. DOI: 10.1177/1350508405057474

Arts Council England (2021a) *Let's Create. Strategy 2020–2030*, London: Arts Council England. www.artscouncil.org.uk/lets-create/strategy-2020-2030 [Accessed 18 Dec 2021].

Arts Council England (2021b) 'Equality, diversity and inclusion: A data report, 2020–2021'. www.artscouncil.org.uk/equality-diversity-and-inclusion-data-report-2020-2021 [Accessed 27 Jul 2023].

Bacchi, C., and Goodwin, S. (2016) 'Key themes and concepts', in Bacchi, C., and Goodwin, S. (eds) *Poststructural Policy Analysis*, New York: Palgrave Macmillan US, pp. 27–53.

BAFTA (2020) 'BAFTA 2020 review'. www.bafta.org/about/mission/the-bafta-2020-review

Banks, M. (2017) *Creative Justice: Cultural Industries, Work and Inequality*, London: Rowman & Littlefield International.

Banks, M. (2023) 'Cultural work and contributive justice', *Journal of Cultural Economy*, 16(1), pp. 47–61. DOI: 10.1080/17530350.2022.2058059

BBC (2016) *Diversity and Inclusion Strategy 2016–2020*, London: BBC. http://downloads.bbc.co.uk/diversity/pdf/diversity-and-inclusion-strategy-2016.pdf [Accessed 8 Dec 2021]. (*)

BBC (2017) *Equality Information Report 2016–17*, London: BBC. https://downloads.bbc.co.uk/diversity/pdf/equality-information-report-2017.pdf [Accessed 8 Dec 2021]. (*)

BBC (2018a) *BBC Diversity Commissioning Code of Practice*, London: BBC. http://downloads.bbc.co.uk/diversity/pdf/diversity-code-of-practice-2018.pdf [Accessed 8 Dec 2021]. (*)

BBC (2018b) *Equality Information Report 2017–18*, London: BBC. http://downloads.bbc.co.uk/diversity/pdf/bbc-equality-information-report-2017-18.pdf [Accessed 8 Dec 2021]. (*)

BBC (2018c) *Reflecting the Socio-Economic Diversity of the UK within the BBC Workforce*, London: BBC. http://downloads.bbc.co.uk/diversity/pdf/socio-economic-diversity.pdf [Accessed 8 Dec 2021]. (*)

BBC (2018d) *Reflecting the Ethnic Diversity of the UK within the BBC Workforce*, London: BBC. http://downloads.bbc.co.uk/diversity/pdf/bame-career-progression-and-culture-report.pdf [Accessed 8 Dec 2021]. (*)

BBC (2018e) *Making the BBC a Great Workplace for Women*, London: BBC. http://downloads.bbc.co.uk/aboutthebbc/insidethebbc/reports/gender_equality_recommendations_2018.pdf [Accessed 8 Dec 2021]. (*)

BBC (2018f) *Reflecting Disability in the UK within the BBC Workforce*, London: BBC. https://downloads.bbc.co.uk/mediacentre/reflecting_disability.pdf [Accessed 8 Dec 2021]. (*)

BBC (2018g) *Statutory Gender Pay Gap Report*, London: BBC. http://downloads.bbc.co.uk/aboutthebbc/insidethebbc/reports/gender_pay_report_2018.pdf [Accessed 8 Dec 2021]. (*)

BBC (2018h) *LGBT Culture and Progression: A Report on Career Progression and Culture at the BBC*, London: BBC. www.bbc.co.uk/diversity/reports/lgbt-culture-and-progression/ [Accessed 7 Aug 2023]. (*)

BBC (2019a) *BBC Diversity Commissioning Code of Practice Progress Report*, London: BBC. http://downloads.bbc.co.uk/aboutthebbc/reports/reports/diversity-cop-progress-1920.pdf [Accessed 8 Dec 2021]. (*)

BBC (2019b) *Making the BBC a Great Workplace for Women*, London: BBC. http://downloads.bbc.co.uk/diversity/pdf/making-the-bbc-a-great-workplace-for-women.pdf [Accessed 8 Dec 2021]. (*)

BBC (2019c) *Gender Pay Gap Report*, London: BBC. http://downloads.bbc.co.uk/aboutthebbc/reports/reports/gender-pay-gap-2019.pdf [Accessed 8 Dec 2021]. (*)

BBC (2019d) *Reflecting the Ethnic Diversity of the UK within the BBC Workforce*, London: BBC. http://downloads.bbc.co.uk/diversity/pdf/bame-career-progression-and-culture-report.pdf [Accessed 8 Dec 2021]. (*)

BBC (2020) 'Gender pay gap'. https://downloads.bbc.co.uk/aboutthebbc/reports/reports/pay-gap-report-2020.pdf [Accessed 7 Aug 2023]. (*)

BBC (2021a) *50:50 Project Impact Report 2021*, London: BBC. www.bbc.com/5050/documents/50-50-impact-report-2021.pdf [Accessed 8 Dec 2021]. (*)

BBC (2021b) *Diversity and Inclusion Plan 2021–2023*, London: BBC. www.bbc.com/diversity/documents/bbc-diversity-and-inclusion-plan20-23.pdf [Accessed 8 Dec 2021]. (*)

BBC (2022a) *Diversity Commissioning Code of Practice Progress Report 2021/22*, London: BBC. www.bbc.co.uk/creativediversity/documents/bbc-diversity-code-of-practice-2021-2022.pdf [Accessed 7 Aug 2023]. (*)

BBC (2022b) *50:50 Project Impact Report 2022*, London: BBC. www.bbc.co.uk/5050/documents/5050-impact-report-2022.pdf [Accessed 7 Aug 2023]. (*)

BBC (2022c) *Equality Information Report 21/22*, London: BBC. www.bbc.co.uk/aboutthebbc/documents/equality-information-report-2022.pdf [Accessed 7 Aug 2023]. (*)

BBC (n.d.) *£100 Million TV Commissioning Spend. Prioritising Diverse Content and People in Our Commissioning*, London: BBC. www.bbc.co.uk/commissioning/diversity-100-million-spend [Accessed 8 Dec 2021].

BBC/Sir Lenny Henry Centre for Media Diversity (2021) *BAME Terminology Review Report*, Birmingham: Birmingham City University. www.bbc.co.uk/diversity/reports/bame-terminology-review/ [Accessed 7 Aug 2023]. (*)

BBC Studios (2021) *Pay Gap Report*, London: BBC Studios. www.bbcstudios.com/media/4700/bbc-studios-pay-gap-report-2021-final.pdf [Accessed 7 Aug 2023]. (*)

Benjamin, R. (2022) *Viral Justice. How We Grow the World We Want*, Princeton: Princeton University Press.

BFI (2017) *BFI2022. Supporting UK Film. BFI Plan 2017–2022*, London BFI. https://www2.bfi.org.uk/2022/downloads/bfi2022_EN.pdf [Accessed 8 Dec 2021]. (*)

BFI (2019) *Diversity Standards*, London: BFI. www.bfi.org.uk/inclusion-film-industry/bfi-diversity-standards [Accessed 8 Dec 2021]. (*)

BFI (2020a) 'Set of principles: To tackle and prevent bullying, harassment and racism in the screen industries'. file:///C:/Users/User/Downloads/bfi-principles-tackle-and-prevent-bullying-harassment-racism-screen-industries-2021-03-17.pdf [Accessed 12 Jun 2023].

BFI (2020b) 'Guidance: A practical workplace guide for the prevention of bullying, harassment and racism in the screen industries'. file:///C:/Users/User/Downloads/bfi-bullying-and-harassment-and-racism-guidance-2020-09-16-v1.pdf [Accessed 12 Jun 2023].

BFI (2020c) *BFI Diversity Standards Initial Findings. Production June 2016–March 2019*, London: BFI. https://www2.bfi.org.uk/sites/bfi.org.uk/files/downloads/bfi-diversity-standards-initial-findings-production-june-2016-march-2019-v1.pdf [Accessed 8 Dec 2021]. (*)

BFI (2022) *Review of the Diversity Standards: A Summary of Industry Perspectives and Recommendations*, London: BFI. www.bfi.org.uk/industry-data-insights/reports/review-bfi-diversity-standards [Accessed 7 Aug 2023]. (*)

BFI (n.d.) *Inclusion Targets*, London: BFI. www.bfi.org.uk/inclusion-film-industry/inclusion-targets [Accessed 15 Dec 2021].

Boxenbaum, E., and Jonsson, S. (2017) 'Isomorphism, diffusion and decoupling: Concept evolution and theoretical challenges', in Greenwood, R., Oliver, C., Lawrence, T. B., and Meyer, R. E. (eds) *The SAGE Handbook of Organizational Institutionalism*, 2nd ed., London: SAGE, pp. 77–101.

Bryman, A. (2016) *Social Research Methods*, 5th ed., Oxford: Oxford University Press.

Business in the Community (BITC) (2020) *Race at Work Charter Report*, London: BITC. www.bitc.org.uk/wp-content/uploads/2020/10/bitc-report-race-raceatwork chartersurvey2020-Oct20.pdf [Accessed 15 Dec 2021].

CAMEo (2018) *Workforce Diversity in the UK Screen Sector: Evidence Review*, Leicester: CAMEo Research Institute. www.bfi.org.uk/industry-data-insights/reports/workforce-diversity-uk-screen-sector-evidence-review [Accessed 15 Dec 2021].

CAMEo (2019) *Doubling Disability Research Report*, Leicester: CAMEo Research Institute. https://creativediversitynetwork.com/wp-content/uploads/2019/12/Doubling-Disability-Trifold-Black-Font.pdf [Accessed 17 Dec 2021].

Carey, H., Florisson, R., O Brien, D., and Lee, N. (2020) 'Getting in and getting on class, participation, and job quality in the UK Creative Industries. Policy Review Series: Class in the Creative industries – Paper No.01'. www.pec.ac.uk/assets/publications/PEC-report-class-in-the-creative-industries-FINAL.pdf [Accessed 15 Dec 2021].

Carey, H., O'Brien, D., and Gable, O. (2021) 'Screened out. Tackling class inequality in the UK Screen Industries'. www.pec.ac.uk/assets/publications/PEC-and-ScreenSkills-report-Screened-Out-FINAL-April-2021.pdf [Accessed 17 Dec 2021].

Carty, M. (2020) *Diversity and Inclusion Survey 2020*, London: XpertHR. www.xperthr.co.uk/survey-analysis/diversity-and-inclusion-survey-2020/165151/ [Accessed 27 Jul 2023].

CDN (2020) *Diamond. The Third Cut*, London: CDN. https://creativediversitynetwork.com/wp-content/uploads/2020/02/CDN_Diamond_25Feb.pdf [Accessed 8 Dec 2021]. (*)

CDN (2021) *Diamond. The Fourth Cut*, London: CDN. https://creativediversitynetwork.com/wp-content/uploads/2021/01/CDN-Diamond4-JANUARY-27-FINAL.pdf [Accessed 15 Dec 2021].

CDN (2022) *The Fifth Cut: Diamond at 5*, London: CDN. https://creativediversitynetwork.com/diamond/diamond-reports/the-fifth-cut-diamond-at-5/ [Accessed 27 Jul 2023]. (*)

CDN (2023) *Diamond. The Sixth Cut*, London: CDN. https://creativediversitynetwork.com/wp-content/uploads/2023/07/Diamond-The-6th-Cut-July2023.pdf [Accessed 13 Jul 2023].

CDN (n.d.) *Doubling Disability*, London: CDN. https://creativediversitynetwork.com/doubling-disability/understanding-the-problem/ [Accessed 15 Dec 2021].

Channel 4 (2015) *360° Diversity Charter*, London: Channel 4. www.channel4.com/media/documents/corporate/diversitycharter/Channel4360DiversityCharterFINAL.pdf [Accessed 8 Dec 2021]. (*)

Channel 4 (2017) *360° Diversity Charter – Two Years On*, London: Channel 4. www.channel4.com/media/documents/corporate/26509_C4_DiversityReport2017_FINAL_27.02.17.pdf [Accessed 8 Dec 2021]. (*)

Channel 4 (2018) *360° Diversity Charter – Three Years On*, London: Channel 4. https://assets-corporate.channel4.com/_flysystem/s3/2018-05/Channel%204%20-%20360%20Diversity%20Charter%20-%20Three%20Years%20On_FINAL_4.pdf [Accessed 8 Dec 2021]. (*)

Channel 4 (2019a) *Inclusion & Diversity: Strategy & Targets*, London: Channel 4. https://assets-corporate.channel4.com/_flysystem/s3/2019-11/Channel%204%20-%20Inclusion%20and%20Diversity%20Strategy%202019_7.pdf [Accessed 8 Dec 2021]. (*)

Channel 4 (2019b) *Fourteen Insights into Inclusion and Diversity*, London: Channel 4. https://s3-eu-west-1.amazonaws.com/c4-cp-assets/corporate-assets/2019-10/Channel%204%20-%20Inclusion%20%26%20Diversity%20Insights%20-%20October%202019.pdf [Accessed 15 Dec 2021].

Channel 4 (2019c) *RISE. A Review of Channel 4's Women's Development Programme*, London: Channel 4. https://s3-eu-west-1.amazonaws.com/c4-cp-assets/

corporate-assets/2019-01/CHA001_RISE_whitepaper_080119_6.pdf [Accessed 8 Dec 2021]. (*)

Channel 4 (2021a) *Channel 4's Commissioning Diversity Guidelines*, London: Channel 4. https://assets-corporate.channel4.com/_flysystem/s3/documents/2021-07/CommissioningDiversityGuidelines_ResourcesAndContacts_202107.pdf [Accessed 15 Dec 2021].

Channel 4 (2021b) *Guide to Hiring Disabled Talent in the TV Industry*, London: Channel 4. https://assets-corporate.channel4.com/_flysystem/s3/2021-11/38793_Channel4_DisabilityGuide_Hiring_PLAIN_TEXT_AW.pdf [Accessed 7 Aug 2023]. (*)

Channel 4 (2021c) *Guide to Including Disabled Talent in the TV Industry*, London: Channel 4. https://assets-corporate.channel4.com/_flysystem/s3/2021-11/38793_Channel4_DisabilityGuide_Including.pdf [Accessed 7 Aug 2023]. (*)

Channel 4 (2021d) *Guide to Progressing Disabled Talent in the TV Industry*, London: Channel 4. https://assets-corporate.channel4.com/_flysystem/s3/2021-11/38793_Channel4_DisabilityGuide_Progressing.pdf [Accessed 7 Aug 2023]. (*)

Channel 4 (2022a) *Channel Four Television Corporation Pay Report 2022*, London: Channel 4. https://assets-corporate.channel4.com/_flysystem/s3/2022-10/221005%20-%20Pay%20Report%202022%20-%20FINAL.pdf [Accessed 7 Aug 2023].

Channel 4 (2022b) *Commissioning Diversity Guidelines*, London: Channel 4. https://assets-corporate.channel4.com/_flysystem/s3/documents/2022-06/Channel%204%20-%202022%20Commissioning%20Diversity%20Guidelines%20-%20FINAL%20%28Accessible%29.pdf [Accessed 7 Aug 2023]. (*)

Channel 4/Graeme Whippy (2018) *Employing Disabled Talent. A Guide for the TV Sector*, London: Channel 4. https://s3-eu-west-1.amazonaws.com/c4-cp-assets/corporate-assets/documents/2018-02/TV%20Sector%20Guide%20to%20Employing%20Disabled%20Talent_Version1.pdf [Accessed 8 Dec 2021]. (*)

CIC (2020) *Creative Industries Council Diversity and Inclusion Progress Report 2019/20*, London: CIC. https://cic-media.s3.eu-west-2.amazonaws.com/media/557057/v24-july-final-draft-cic-diversity-and-inclusion-progress-report-2019-20-2.pdf [Accessed 27 Jul 2023].

CIPD (2015) *Quotas and Targets: How Do They Affect Diversity Progress?*, London: CIPD. www.cipd.co.uk/Images/quotas-and-targets_june-2015-how-affect-diversity-progress_tcm18-10824.pdf [Accessed 15 Dec 2021].

CIPD (2018) *Diversity and Inclusion at Work. Facing Up to the Business Case*, London: CIPD. www.cipd.co.uk/knowledge/fundamentals/relations/diversity/diversity-inclusion-report#grefn [Accessed 15 Dec 2021].

CIPD (2019) *Diversity Management That Works. An Evidence-Based View*, London: CIPD. www.cipd.co.uk/Images/7926-diversity-and-inclusion-report-revised_tcm18-65334.pdf [Accessed 25 Dec 2021].

Cobb, S. (2020) 'What about the men? Gender inequality data and the rhetoric of inclusion in the US and UK film industries', *Journal of British Cinema and Television*, 17(1), pp. 112–135. DOI: 10.3366/jbctv.2020.0510

Coles, A., and Eikhof, D. R. (2021) 'On the basis of risk: How screen executives' risk perceptions and practices drive gender inequality in directing', *Gender, Work and Organisation*, 28(6), pp. 2040–2057. DOI: 10.1111/gwao.12701

Coles, A., MacNeill, K., Vincent, J. B., Vincent, C., and Barre, P. (2018) *The Status of Women in the Canadian Arts and Cultural Industries: Research Review 2010–2018. Prepared for the Ontario Arts Council*, Melbourne: Deakin University. www.arts.on.ca/oac/media/oac/Publications/Research%20Reports%20EN-FR/Arts%20

Funding%20and%20Support/OAC-Women-the-Arts-Report_Final_EN_Oct5.pdf [Accessed 15 Dec 2021].

Creative Equity Toolkit (n.d.) 'Set diversity targets'. https://creativeequitytoolkit.org/topic/programming-commissioning/set-diversity-targets/ [Accessed 15 Dec 2021].

Creative Industries Councils (forthcoming) *Charting Progress Framework*.

Creative Scotland (2022) 'Creative Scotland equality outcomes 2022–26'. www.creativescotland.com/__data/assets/pdf_file/0006/92355/Equality-Outcomes-2022-2026.pdf [Accessed 27 Jul 2023].

Creative Skillset (2015) *Making TV More Diverse*, London: ScreenSkills. www.ScreenSkills.com/media/1561/ss8359_tv_diversity_booklet_v6.pdf [Accessed 8 Dec 2021]. (*)

Crenshaw, K. (1989) 'Demarginalizing the intersection of race and sex: A black feminist critique of antidiscrimination doctrine, feminist theory and antiracist politics', *University of Chicago Legal Forum*, (1), Article 8. http://chicagounbound.uchicago.edu/uclf/vol1989/iss1/8 [Accessed 7 Dec 2021].

Criado Perez, C. (2019) *Invisible Women. Exposing Data Bias in a World Designed for Men*, London: Penguin Random House.

Dabiri, E. (2021) *What White People Can Do Next. From Allyship to Coalition*, London: Penguin Random House.

Davies Review (2011) 'Women on boards February 2011'. https://ftsewomenleaders.com/wp-content/uploads/2015/08/women-on-boards-review.pdf [Accessed 15 Dec 2021].

Denis, E. (2022) *Enhancing Gender Diversity on Boards and in Senior Management of Listed Companies, Report for OECD*. https://www.oecd.org/corporate/ca/enhancing-gender-diversity-on-boards-and-in-senior-management-of-listed-companies-4f7ca695-en.htm [Accessed 2 Oct 2023].

D'Ignazio, C., and Klein, L. (2020) *Data Feminism*, Cambridge: MIT Press.

Eddo-Lodge, R. (2018) *Why I'm No Longer Talking to White People About Race*, London: Bloomsbury.

Eikhof, D. R. (2014) 'The transorganisational context of creative production: Challenges for individuals and management', in Bilton, C., and Cummings, S. (eds) *Handbook of Management and Creativity*, Cheltenham: Edward Elgar, pp. 275–297.

Eikhof, D. R. (2019) 'Statistics vs evidence: Improving diversity in the screen industries', *Diamond Xchange*. www.youtube.com/watch?v=Zu-lVyhLLu0 [Accessed 13 Jul 2023].

Eikhof, D. R., Guyan, K., Coles, A., and Williams, C. (forthcoming) *Gender Equity Policy in the Canadian, German and UK Film*.

Eikhof, D. R., Newsinger, J., Luchinskaya, D., and Aidley, D. (2019) 'And . . . action? Gender, knowledge and inequalities in the UK screen industries', *Gender, Work & Organization*, 26(6), pp. 840–859. DOI: 10.1111/gwao.12318

European Institute for Gender Equality (EIGE) (2018) *Gender-Balanced Participation*, Vilnius: EIGE. https://eige.europa.eu/thesaurus/terms/1149 [Accessed 15 Dec 2021].

Film and TV Charity (n.d.) 'The whole picture toolkit'. https://filmtvcharity.org.uk/your-support/support-for-employers/the-whole-picture-toolkit/ [Accessed 12 Jun 2023].

GDPR EU (2023) 'GDPR: General data protection regulation'. www.gdpreu.org/ [Accessed 19 Aug 2023].

Golightley, M., and Holloway, M. (2017) 'To boldly struggle where once we aspired to go: Disability today', *The British Journal of Social Work*, 47(3), pp. 601–610. DOI: 10.1093/bjsw/bcx043

Gov.uk (2023) 'The Data Protection Act'. www.gov.uk/data-protection [Accessed 19 Aug 2023].

Government Equalities Office (2023a) 'Statutory guidance: Report your gender pay gap data'. www.gov.uk/government/publications/gender-pay-gap-reporting-guidance-for-employers/report-your-gender-pay-gap-data#:~:text=You%20must%20report%20your%20gender,their%20gender%20pay%20gap%20data [Accessed 23 Jun 2023].

Government Equalities Office (2023b) 'Guidance: Positive action in the workplace'. www.gov.uk/government/publications/positive-action-in-the-workplace-guidance-for-employers/positive-action-in-the-workplace#implementing-positive-action-lawfully-checklist-for-employers [Accessed 28 Jun 2023].

Grote, D. (2017) '3 popular goal-setting techniques managers should avoid', *Harvard Business Review*, 2 Jan. https://hbr.org/2017/01/3-popular-goal-setting-techniques-managers-should-avoid [Accessed 19 Aug 2023].

Guyan, K. (2021a) 'For queer communities, being counted has downsides', *Wired*, 15 Dec. www.wired.com/story/queer-data-census-equality/ [Accessed 27 Jul 2023].

Guyan, K. (2021b) 'Constructing a queer population? Asking about sexual orientation in Scotland's 2022 census', *Journal of Gender Studies*, 31(6), pp. 782–792. DOI: 10.1080/09589236.2020.1866513

Guyan, K. (2022) *Queer Data. Using Gender, Sex and Sexuality for Action*, London: Bloomsbury.

Guyan, K., and Eikhof, D. R. (forthcoming) *LGBQ+ Data and Workforce Diversity*.

HM Government (2021) 'National disability strategy'. www.gov.uk/government/publications/national-disability-strategy [Accessed 27 Jul 2023].

House of Commons Library (2023) 'Disabled people in employment: Research briefing'. https://researchbriefings.files.parliament.uk/documents/CBP-7540/CBP-7540.pdf [Accessed 18 Aug 2023].

ITN (2018a) *ITN BAME Pay Gap Report 2018*, London: ITN. www.itn.co.uk/wp-content/uploads/2018/07/ITN-BAME-Pay-Report-2018.pdf [Accessed 8 Dec 2021]. (*)

ITN (2018b) *ITN Gender Pay Gap Report 2017–2018*, London: ITN. www.itn.co.uk/wp-content/uploads/2018/11/ITN-Gender-Pay-Report-2017-2018.pdf [Accessed 8 Dec 2021]. (*)

ITN (2019) *ITN Gender and Ethnicity Pay Gap Report 2018–2019*, London: ITN. www.itn.co.uk/wp-content/uploads/2019/10/ITN-Gender-and-Ethnicity-Pay-Report-2018-2019.pdf [Accessed 8 Dec 2021]. (*)

ITN (2023) *New Diversity and Inclusion Report 2023*, London: ITN. www.itn.co.uk/sites/default/files/2023-04/ITN%20Diversity%20and%20Inclusion%20Report%202023%20For%20Site.pdf [Accessed 7 Aug 2023]. (*)

ITV (2018) *ITV's Commission Commitments Overview*, London: ITV. www.itv-plc.com/~/media/Files/I/ITV-PLC/download/itv-commissioning-commitments-overview.pdf [Accessed 8 Dec 2021]. (*)

ITV (2019) *ITV Social Purpose Impact Report*, London: ITV. www.itvplc.com/~/media/Files/I/ITV-PLC/download/itv-social-purpose-impact-report-2019.pdf [Accessed 8 Dec 2021]. (*)

ITV (2020) *ITV Social Purpose Impact Report*, London: ITV. www.itvplc.com/~/media/Files/I/ITV-PLC/download/itv-social-purpose-report-2020.pdf [Accessed 8 Dᴏᴏ 2021]. (*)

ITV (2021) *New Diversity Acceleration Plan Report 2021*, London: ITV. www.itv.com/inclusion/articles/diversity-acceleration-plan [Accessed 7 Aug 2023]. (*)

ITV (2022a) *ITV Social Purpose Impact Report 2022*, London: ITV. www.itvplc.com/~/media/Files/I/ITV-PLC/download/2022-itv-social-purpose-report.pdf [Accessed 27 Jul 2023]. (*)

ITV (2022b) *New Diversity Acceleration Plan Report 2022*, London: ITV. www.itv.com/inclusion/articles/diversity-acceleration-plan [Accessed 7 Aug 2023]. (*)

Jaishiv, A. J. (2022) 'The missing theory for regulation and law-making: Women in corporate leadership', *Journal of Corporate Law Studies*, 22(2), pp. 807–841. DOI: 10.1080/14735970.2022.2156203

Kang, W., Ashton, J. K., Orujov, A., and Wang, Y. (2023) 'Realizing gender diversity on corporate boards', *International Journal of the Economics of Business*, 30(1), pp. 1–29. DOI: 10.1080/13571516.2022.2133337

Katsha, H. (2023) 'Baftas 2023: All the winners were white and yes, people noticed', *Huffington Post*, 20 Feb. www.huffingtonpost.co.uk/entry/baftas-2023-all-the-winners-were-white-and-yes-people-noticed_uk_63f33904e4b0c87f32f246ed [Accessed 3 Jul 2023].

Law, J., Ruppert, E., and Savage, M. (2011) *The Double Social Life of Methods (CRESC Working Paper Series, Working Paper No. 95)*, Milton Keynes: CRESC. https://research.gold.ac.uk/id/eprint/7987/1/The%20Double%20Social%20Life%20of%20Methods%20CRESC%20Working%20Paper%2095.pdf [Accessed 13 Jul 2023].

Lowder, B., Gill-Peterson, J., and Cauterucci, C. (2023) 'The trans past, present, and future', *Outward: Slate's LGBTQ Podcast* [podcast]. https://slate.com/podcasts/outward/2022/03/trans-past-present-future [Accessed 17 Aug 2013].

Maxwell, G. A. (2004) 'Minority report: Taking the initiative in managing diversity at BBC Scotland', *Employee Relations*, 26(2), pp. 182–202. DOI: 10.1108/1425450410511089

McGregor-Smith Review (2017) *Race in the Workplace: The McGregor-Smith Review – Annexes*, London: Department for Business, Energy and Industrial Strategy. www.gov.uk/government/publications/race-in-the-workplace-the-mcgregor-smith-review/race-in-the-workplace-the-mcgregor-smith-review-annexes#a-best-practice-case-studies [Accessed 15 Dec 2021].

Mensi-Klarbach, H., Leixnering, S., and Schifnger, M. (2021) 'The carrot or the stick: self-regulation for gender-diverse boards via codes of good governance', *Journal of Business Ethics*, 170, pp. 577–593. DOI: 10.1007/s10551-019-04336-z

Menzies, F. (2018) *Meaningful Metrics for Diversity and Inclusion*, Sydney: Culture Plus Consulting. https://cultureplusconsulting.com/2018/10/16/meaning-metrics-for-diversity-and-inclusion/ [Accessed 15 Dec 2021].

Myers, V. (2014) 'How to overcome our biases? Walk boldly toward them', *Ted Talk* [video]. www.ted.com/talks/verna_myers_how_to_overcome_our_biases_walk_boldly_toward_them/transcript?language=en [Accessed 27 Jul 2023].

Noon, M., and Ogbonna, E. (2021) 'Controlling management to deliver diversity and inclusion: Prospects and limits', *Human Resource Management Journal*, 31, pp. 619–638. DOI: 10.1111/1748-8583.12332

Ofcom (2017a) *Diversity and Inclusion at Ofcom*, London: Ofcom. www.ofcom.org.uk/__ data/assets/pdf_file/0023/106664/diversity-report-2017.pdf [Accessed 8 Dec 2021]. (*)

Ofcom (2017b) *Diversity and Equal Opportunities in Television. Monitoring Report on the UK-Based Broadcasting Industry*, London: Ofcom. www.ofcom.org.uk/__data/ assets/pdf_file/0017/106343/diversity-television-report-2017.pdf [Accessed 8 Dec 2021]. (*)

Ofcom (2018a) *Ofcom's Diversity and Inclusion Programme 2018–2022*, London: Ofcom. www.ofcom.org.uk/__data/assets/pdf_file/0009/112500/dip-statement.pdf [Accessed 8 Dec 2021]. (*)

Ofcom (2018b) *Diversity and Equal Opportunities in Television. Monitoring Report on the UK-Based Broadcasting Industry*, London: Ofcom. www.ofcom.org.uk/__data/ assets/pdf_file/0021/121683/diversity-in-TV-2018-report.PDF [Accessed 8 Dec 2021]. (*)

Ofcom (2019a) *Ofcom's Annual Gender-Ethnicity Pay Audit 2018/19*, London: Ofcom. www.ofcom.org.uk/__data/assets/pdf_file/0022/142294/ofcom-annual-gender-ethnicity-pay-audit-2018-19.pdf [Accessed 8 Dec 2021]. (*)

Ofcom (2019b) *Diversity in UK Television: Freelancers*, London: Ofcom. www.ofcom. org.uk/__data/assets/pdf_file/0025/166804/diversity-in-tv-2019-freelancers.pdf [Accessed 8 Dec 2021]. (*)

Ofcom (2019c) *Diversity and Inclusion Programme Update 2018/19*, London: Ofcom. www.ofcom.org.uk/__data/assets/pdf_file/0021/158511/diversity-and-inclusion-progress-report-2018-19.pdf [Accessed 8 Dec 2021]. (*)

Ofcom (2020a) *Overview of Ofcom's Diversity in Broadcasting Remit*, London: Ofcom. www.ofcom.org.uk/tv-radio-and-on-demand/information-for-industry/guidance/ diversity/ofcoms-role/overview-of-diversity-in-broadcasting-remit [Accessed 17 Dec 2021].

Ofcom (2020b) *Diversity and Equal Opportunities in Television and Radio 2019/20. Report on the UK-Based Broadcasting Industry*, London: Ofcom. www.ofcom.org.uk/__ data/assets/pdf_file/0022/207229/2019-20-report-diversity-equal-opportunities-tv-and-radio.pdf [Accessed 15 Dec 2021]. (*)

Ofcom (2021a) 'Five-year review: Diversity and equal opportunities in UK broadcasting'. www.ofcom.org.uk/__data/assets/pdf_file/0029/225992/dib-five-years-2021.pdf [Accessed 27 Jul 2023]. (*)

Ofcom (2021b) 'Diversity and equal opportunities in broadcasting 2021: Methodology'. www.ofcom.org.uk/__data/assets/pdf_file/0030/225993/dib-five-years-2021-methodology.pdf [Accessed 27 Jul 2023]. (*)

Ofcom (2021c) *Diversity at Ofcom 2020/21 and Pay Gap 2020/21 Report*, London: Ofcom. www.ofcom.org.uk/__data/assets/pdf_file/0018/222633/diversity-pay-gap-report-20-21.pdf [Accessed 7 Aug 2023]. (*)

Ofcom (2021d) *Making Ofcom Work for Everyone: Ofcom's Diversity and Inclusion Strategy*, London: Ofcom. www.ofcom.org.uk/__data/assets/pdf_file/0012/210900/ diversity-and-inclusion-strategy-report-2019-20.pdf [Accessed 7 Aug 2023]. (*)

Ofcom (2022a) *Diversity and Inclusion Strategy Progress Update 2021/22*, London: Ofcom www.ofcom.org.uk/__data/assets/pdf_file/0029/241868/2021-22-diversity-inclusion-progress-update.pdf [Accessed 7 Aug 2023]. (*)

Ofcom (2022b) *Equity, Diversity and Inclusion in Television and Radio 2021–22*, London: Ofcom. www.ofcom.org.uk/__data/assets/pdf_file/0029/246854/2021-22-report-diversity-in-tv-and-radio.pdf [Accessed 7 Aug 2023]. (*)

Oldford, E. (2022) 'Soft regulation of women on boards: Evidence from Canada', *Business and Society Review*, 127(4), pp. 779–808. DOI: 10.1111/basr.12294

ONS (2023a) 'Annual population survey'. www.ons.gov.uk/employmentandlabourmarket/peopleinwork/employmentandemployeetypes/methodologies/annualpopulationsurveyapsqmi [Accessed 27 Jul 2023].

ONS (2023b) 'Census'. www.ons.gov.uk/census [Accessed 27 Jul 2023].

ONS (2023c) 'Labour force survey'. www.ons.gov.uk/surveys/informationforhouseholds andindividuals/householdandindividualsurveys/labourforcesurvey [Accessed 27 Jul 2023].

Ozimek, A. M. (2020) *Equality, Diversity and Inclusion in the Screen Industries. Scoping Report*, York: University of York. https://eprints.whiterose.ac.uk/170698/1/EDI_report.pdf [Accessed 15 Dec 2021].

PA (2022) *UK Publishing Workforce: Diversity, Inclusion and Belonging*, London: PA. www.publishers.org.uk/publications/diversity-survey-of-the-publishing-workforce-2021/ [Accessed 27 Jul 2023].

Parker Review (2017) 'A report into the ethnic diversity of UK boards: Final report'. https://assets.ey.com/content/dam/ey-sites/ey-com/en_uk/news/2020/02/ey-parker-review-2017-report-final.pdf [Accessed 15 Dec 2021].

Powell, A. (2021) *Disabled People in Employment* (Briefing Paper No. 7540, 24 May), London: House of Commons. https://researchbriefings.files.parliament.uk/documents/CBP-7540/CBP-7540.pdf [Accessed 15 Dec 2021].

PwC (n.d.) 'Diversity data guide. Collecting and analysing data on the inclusion and diversity of your workforce'. https://insights.theia.org/story/ia-diversity-data-guide/page/1 [Accessed 15 Dec 2021].

Reeves, M., and Fuller, J. (2018) 'When SMART goals are not so smart', *MIT Sloan Management Review*, 59(4), pp. 1–5.

Risberg, A., Mensi-Klarback, H., and Hanappi-Egger, E. (2019) 'Setting the scene for diversity in organizations', in Mensi-Klarbach, H., and Risberg, A. (eds) *Diversity in Organizations. Concepts and Practices*, 2nd ed., London: Red Globe Press, pp. 3–30.

S4C (2015) *2015 Report on the Effectiveness of Equality and Diversity Policies and Training and S4C's Compliance with the General Equality Duty under the Equality Act 2010*, Cardiff: S4C. www.s4c.cymru/abouts4c/diversity/pdf/2015-report-on-the-effectiveness-of-equality-and-diversity-policies-and-training-and-s4c-compliance-with-the-general-equality-duty-under-the-equality-act-2010.pdf [Accessed 8 Dec 2021]. (*)

S4C (2016a) *Commitment to Equality and Diversity– April 2016*, Cardiff: S4C. https://dlo6cycw1kmbs.cloudfront.net/media/media_assets/2016.04.07_S4C_Diversity_Committment_-_Final_-_Clean.pdf [Accessed 15 Dec 2021]. (*)

S4C (2016b) *Diversity, Equality and Equal Opportunities Policy – June 2016*, Cardiff: S4C. www.s4c.cymru/abouts4c/authority/pdf/2016.06.20%20Code%20of%20Conduct%20-%20Diversity%20Equality%20and%20Equal%20Opportunities%20Policy.pdf [Accessed 8 Dec 2021]. (*)

S4C (2018a) *Commitment to Equality and Diversity 2018–2021*, Cardiff: S4C. https://dlo6cycw1kmbs.cloudfront.net/media/media_assets/ymrwymiad-amrywiaeth-diversity-commitment-2018.pdf [Accessed 7 Aug 2023]. (*)

S4C (2018b) *Diversity, Equality and Equal Opportunities Policy – July 2018*, Cardiff: S4C. https://dlo6cycw1kmbs.cloudfront.net/media/media_assets/2018_12_05_

Code_of_Conduct_-_Diversity_Equality_and_Equal_Opportunities_Policy.pdf [Accessed 8 Dec 2021]. (*)

S4C (2021a) *Diversity, Equality, Equal Opportunity and Inclusion Policy – June 2021*, Cardiff: S4C. https://dlo6cycw1kmbs.cloudfront.net/media/media_assets/Diversity_ Equality_Equal_Opportunities_and_Inclusion_Policy_S4C_Final_2021_EN.pdf [Accessed 7 Aug 2023]. (*)

S4C (2021b) *New Diversity and Inclusion Action Plan 2021–2025*, Cardiff: S4C. https://dlo6cycw1kmbs.cloudfront.net/media/media_assets/Diversity_and_Inclu- sion_Action_Plan_S4C_Final_2021_EN.pdf [Accessed 7 Aug 2023]. (*)

S4C (2022) *S4C's Compliance with and Application of the General Equality Duty (Under the Equality Act 2010): 2020–2021 Report*, Cardiff: S4C. https://dlo6cycw1kmbs. cloudfront.net/media/media_assets/2020-2021_PSED_Report_S4C_310322.pdf [Accessed 7 Aug 2023]. (*)

Saha, A. (2010) ' "Beards, scarves, halal meat, terrorists, forced marriage": Televi- sion industries and the production of "race" ', *Media, Culture & Society*, 34(4), pp. 424–438.

ScreenSkills (2019a) *Annual ScreenSkills Assessment*, London: ScreenSkills. www. ScreenSkills.com/media/2853/2019-08-16-annual-ScreenSkills-assessment.pdf [Accessed 8 Dec 2021]. (*)

ScreenSkills (2019b) *Monitoring Diversity and Inclusion*, London: ScreenSkills. www. ScreenSkills.com/about-us/diversity-and-inclusivity/guide-to-diversity-and-inclusivity- monitoring/ [Accessed 15 Dec 2021].

Screenskills (2021) *Annual Screenskills Assessment 2021*, London: Screenskills. www.screenskills.com/media/4587/2021-06-08-screenskills-assessment-2021.pdf [Accessed 7 Aug 2023]. (*)

ScreenSkills (2023) *D&I Targets Playbook*, ScreenSkills & University of Glasgow. www.screenskills.com/media/7721/screenskills-d-and-i-playbook-june-2023.pdf [Accessed 13 Jul 2023].

Seramount (2017) 'Setting and achieving diversity targets updated 8/2017'. www. diversitybestpractices.com/about-diversity-best-practices [Accessed 15 Dec 2021].

Sky (2020) *Diversity Guidance Notice for Production Companies, 1st October 2020*, London: Sky. https://static.skyassets.com/contentstack/assets/bltdc2476c7b6b194dd/ blt7d4a9e43b667c8b3/5f896c5bdcf0e74b7cbf6ad9/Sky_Diversity_Guidance_ Note_-_1_Oct_20_(002).pdf

Sky (2021a) *Bigger Picture Impact Report 2020*, London: Sky. https://static.skyassets. com/contentstack/assets/bltdc2476c7b6b194dd/blt413353949e85b2cd/Sky_ Impact_Report_2020_Seeing_the_Bigger_Picture.pdf [Accessed 8 Dec 2021]. (*)

Sky (2022) *Bigger Picture Impact Report 2021*, London: Sky. https://static.skyassets. com/contentstack/assets/bltdc2476c7b6b194dd/blt94bb0790501859cb/633c3203ed ed0211051c3a30/Impact_Report_2021.pdf [Accessed 7 Aug 2023]. (*)

Stawski, K., Stendel, S., and Bömelburg (2020) 'Wider das Stagma: 40 machtvolle Frauen brechen im stern mit einem Tabu', *Stern Online*, 25 Nov. www.stern.de/ politik/quotenfrauen/quotenfrau–40-machtvolle-frauen-positionieren-sich-im-stern- gegen-das-stigma-9502364.html [Accessed 12 Jul 2023].

Taylor, M. (2022) 'UK Games Industry Census: Understanding diversity in the UK games industry workforce', *UKIE & University of Sheffield*. https://ukie.org.uk/ resources/uk-games-industry-census-2022 [Accessed 27 Jul 2023].

Tulshyan, R. (2022) *Inclusion on Purpose: An Intersectional Approach to Creating a Culture of Belonging at Work*, Cambridge: MIT Press.

UK Music (2022) *UK Music Diversity Report 2022*, London: UK Music. www.ukmusic.org/equality-diversity/uk-music-diversity-report-2022/ [Accessed 27 Jul 2023].

UK Parliament (2020) 'The public sector equality duty and equality impact assessments'. https://commonslibrary.parliament.uk/research-briefings/sn06591/ [Accessed 18 Aug 2023].

UK Screen Alliance (2019) *Inclusion and Diversity in UK Visual Effects, Animation and Post-Production*, London: UKSA. www.ukscreenalliance.co.uk/subpages/inclusion-and-diversity-in-the-uks-vfx-animation-and-post-production-sectors/ [Accessed 15 Dec 2021].

Viacom/Channel 5 (2016) *Viacom in the UK Diversity and Inclusion Strategy*, London: Viacom.

Vinnicombe, S., Doldor, E., Battista, V., and Tessaro, M. (2020) *The Female FTSE Board Report 2020: Taking Targets Seriously*, Bedford: Cranfield School of Management. www.cranfield.ac.uk/som/research-centres/gender-leadership-and-inclusion-centre/female-ftse-board-report [Accessed 15 Dec 2021].

Viviers, S., Mans-Kemp, N., and Shiel, T. (2022) 'Drivers of board gender diversity in a self-regulatory context', *Management Dynamics*, 31(1), pp. 1–17.

Walby, S. (2011) 'Is the knowledge society gendered?', *Gender, Work and Organization*, 18(1), pp. 1–29. DOI: 10.1111/ j.1468-0432.2010.00532.x

Welsh Government (2021) 'Workforce equality, diversity and inclusion strategy: 2021 to 2026'. www.gov.wales/sites/default/files/pdf-versions/2021/6/5/1623412868/workforce-equality-diversity-and-inclusion-strategy-2021-to-2026.pdf [Accessed 18 Aug 2023].

Work Foundation (2017) *A Skills Audit of the UK Film and Screen Industries*, London: Work Foundation. www.ScreenSkills.com/media/1814/420_a-skills-audit-of-the-uk-film-and-screen-industries.pdf [Accessed 8 Dec 2021]. (*)

Workplace Gender Equality Agency (2013) 'How to set gender diversity targets'. www.wgea.gov.au/sites/default/files/documents/SETTING-GENDER-TARGETS-Online-accessible_0.pdf [Accessed 27 Jul 2023].

Wreyford, N., O'Brien, D., and Dent, T. (2021) 'Creative Majority: An APPG for Creative Diversity report on "What Works" to support, encourage and improve diversity, equity and inclusion in the creative sector. A report for the All Party Parliamentary Group for Creative Diversity'. www.kcl.ac.uk/cultural/resources/reports/creative-majority-report-v2.pdf [Accessed 15 Dec 2021].

Appendices

Appendix 1: The underlying research

Chapters 2–4 of this book draw on and extend the *ScreenSkills D&I Targets Review*, a contract research project led by the University of Glasgow. The *ScreenSkills D&I Targets Review* combined desk-based research, including a rapid evidence review, with stakeholder consultations.

Throughout the book and particularly in Chapter 4, I cite evidence on current and recent D&I practices in the UK screen industries. This evidence is drawn from publicly available reports by BBC, BFI, CDN, Channel 4, ITV, Netflix, Ofcom, Pact, Sky and ViacomCBS. An initial search for the Screen-Skills *D&I Targets Review* identified 51 such publications for the period 2010–2021 published on these organisations' websites. Relevant new publications were added over 2022 and a follow-up website search conducted in early 2023. Up to the completion of the book manuscript, a total of 27 relevant and publicly available sources were identified and included in the analysis. These publications have been marked with (*) in the list of references (Chapter 6).

The topics covered in especially Chapters 2 and 3 required a good grasp on the state of the art in research on D&I targets – in the UK screen and creative industries and beyond. Relevant research and evidence was identified through a rapid evidence review undertaken for the *ScreenSkills D&I Targets Review* and updated in spring 2023.

The initial rapid evidence review targeted research and good practice guidelines in setting diversity and inclusion targets and covered academic and grey literature published in 2010–2021 in the English language. A test run showed that focusing on the Boolean keywords diversity OR inclusion AND target* was too narrow a search strategy as it did not sufficient pertinent hits. The search terms were therefore widened to include (a) diversity OR inclusion AND Film OR TV industry OR screen OR entertainment or, if it needed to be widened further, (b) diversity OR inclusion. The search mechanisms used in the rapid evidence review were (1) databases Assia, Business Source Complete, IBSS and XpertHR as well as Google Scholar; (2) general search engine search; (3) reference tracing from key publications and (4) website search for UK industry bodies and professional associations with a strong remit for diversity and inclusion and/or UK screen. The website search concentrated on reports and good practice case studies and covered the following websites:

ACAS: www.acas.org.uk/
British Film Institute (BFI): www.bfi.org.uk/
CIPD: www.cipd.co.uk/#gref
Creative Equity Toolkit: https://creativeequitytoolkit.org/
Creative Industries Council (CIC): www.thecreativeindustries.co.uk/
Creative Industries Policy and Evidence Centre: www.pec.ac.uk/
Diversity best practices: www.diversitybestpractices.com/
Employers Network for Equality & Inclusion (enei): www.enei.org.uk/
Equality and Human Rights Commission (EHRC): www.equalityhumanrights.
　com/en
Local Government Association: www.local.gov.uk/
Main Broadcasters (BBC, Sky, Channel 4, Channel 5, itv)
Ofcom: ofcom.org.uk/home
Pact: https://diversity.pact.co.uk/
ScreenSkills: www.screenskills.com/

Based on title and abstract (where available), the initial rapid evidence review identified 61 potentially relevant references. Based on full-text reading, 29 references were used for the *ScreenSkills D&I Targets Review*. Handbook articles were excluded from the initial evidence review given time and budget limits.

To ensure that the book captured advances in research since the completion of the rapid evidence review, a follow-up literature search was undertaken in May–June 2023. An updated search of websites for BBC, BBC Studios, BFI, CDN, Channel 4, ScreenSkills, ITN, ITV, Ofcom and S4C, as well as ACAS, CIPD, Creative Equity Toolkit, Creative Industries Council, Creative Industries Policy and Evidence Centre, Diversity best practices, Employers Network for Equality & Inclusion (enei), Equality and Human Rights Commission (EHRC), Local Government Association, Pact, and Work Foundation identified 36 new documents.

An updated literature search undertaken in June 2023, using the search terms (diversity OR inclusion) AND (film OR TV industry OR screen OR entertainment) in title and/or abstract via the databases ASSIA, Business Source Ultimate, IBBS and Google Scholar produced 367 results for 202X-2023, 16 of which were identified as potentially relevant articles after screening. A further literature search of the same databases using the search terms (diversity OR inclusion) AND (target) in title and/or abstract identified 1208 results, out of which only 9 were screened as potentially relevant.

It should be noted that while the search of organisations' websites only covered UK organisations, the database searches covered research of any geographical footprint or origin, as long as it was published in English, in a journal included in the respective databases and published in 2010–2023.

The large number of research that contained some of the keywords but did not fall within the scope of the review (in other words, that were not sufficiently central enough to the topic of D&I targets) is in itself an indicator that evidence on D&I targets is still emerging – in the screen industries and elsewhere.

Appendix 2: Reference data sources for D&I target setting

Reference data source	Diversity characteristics covered	Frequency of data publication	Availability of national/ regional data	Access
UK Census[8]*	Age, disability, ethnicity (and nationality and citizenship), gender identity (trans status/ history in Scotland, question not asked in Northern Ireland), marital status/ civil partnership, religion, sex, sexual orientation	Every 10 years, with Census 2021 (England and Wales) and 2022 (Scotland) data releases from 2022	Detailed data available on nations and regions	Yes, via UK Data Service and publication of statistical bulletins. Some microdata require researcher registration to access
Annual Population Survey	Age, caring responsibilities (reasons for not working/ not working full time), disability, ethnicity (and nationality and citizenship), gender identity, marital status/ civil partnership, religion, sex, sexual orientation, socio-economic status (parents' occupation, respondents' education)	Ongoing data collection with published data updated every 3 months	Detailed data available on nations and regions	Yes, via UK Data Service and publication of statistical bulletins. Some microdata require researcher registration to access.

Reference data source	Diversity characteristics covered	Frequency of data publication	Availability of national/ regional data	Access
Labour Force Survey	Age, caring responsibilities (reasons for not working/not working full time), disability, ethnicity (and nationality and citizenship), gender identity, marital status/ civil partnership, religion, sex, sexual orientation, socio-economic status (parents' occupation, respondents' education)	Ongoing data collection with published data updated every 3 months.	Detailed data available on nations and regions	Yes, via UK Data Service and publication of statistical bulletins. Some microdata require researcher registration to access
Diamond reports	Age, disability, gender, gender identity, race/ ethnicity, sexual orientation	Annually since 2017	Not available	Published as annual report and Excel dataset, free to download from CDN website
Ofcom reports on broadcasters' workforce diversity data	Age, disability, ethnicity, gender, religion, sexual orientation	Annually since 2017	Not available	Published as annual report, free to download from Ofcom website
Ukie Games Industry Workforce Census	Age, caring responsibilities, disability, gender, gender identity, race/ethnicity, sexual orientation, socio-economic background	First in 2019/2020, repeated in 2021/2022	National/ regional data available on where respondents work	Published reports, free to download from Ukie website
UK Screen Alliance Inclusion and diversity in UK visual effects, animation and post-production	Age, caring responsibilities, disability, gender, gender identity, race/ethnicity, sexual orientation, socio-economic background	One-off 2019 survey	National/ regional data available on where respondents work and where they grew up	Published report, free to download from UKSA website

Index

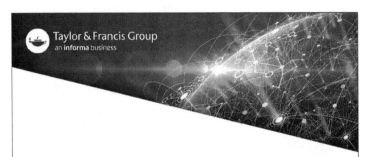

Printed in the United States
by Baker & Taylor Publisher Services